The History of Bêche-de-mer Fishing in Queensland Waters and Adjacent Islands

Paul Dillon

Connor Court Publishing

Published by Connor Court Publishing, 2023.
© Paul Anthony Dillon, 2023.

All rights reserved. No part of this book may be reproduced in any written, electronic, recording, or photocopying without written permission of the publisher or author. The exception would be in the case of brief quotations embodied in the critical articles or reviews and pages where permission is specifically granted by the publisher or author.

Although every precaution has been taken to verify the accuracy of the information contained herein, the author and publisher assume no responsibility for any errors or omissions. No liability is assumed for damages that may result from the use of information contained within.

CONNOR COURT PUBLISHING PTY LTD
PO Box 7257
Redland Bay QLD 4165
sales@connorcourt.com
www.connorcourtpublishing.com.au

ISBN: 9781922815415

Cover design by Maria Giordano

Printed in Australia

Front Cover image: John Oxley Library, State Library of Queensland.

ABOUT THE AUTHOR

Paul Dillon is a Sunshine Coast based author of *Frederick Walker Commandant of the Native Police,* Connor Court Publishing, Brisbane 2018; *The Murder of John Francis Dowling and the Massacre of 300 Aborigines,* Connor Court Publishing, Brisbane 2019; *Inside the Killing Fields Hornet Bank, Cullin-la-Ringo & The Maria Wreck,* Connor Court Publishing, Brisbane 2020; *Queensland Native Police, The First Twenty Years,* 2020; *The Irvinebank Massacre,* Connor Court Publishing, Brisbane 2021; *Fraser Island Massacre Vrai ou Faux,* Connor Court Publishing, Brisbane 2022; *Bêche-de-mer and the Binghis,* 2022; *Dispela Kantri Bilong Mi, Nau! Queensland Annexes New Guinea, 2023;* and *Red Centre, Dead Centre, The True Story of Peter Falconer,* Austin Macauley Publisher, London 2019.

He holds a Bachelor of Arts degree from the Australian National University. Paul joined the Commonwealth Public Service in 1965. On 23 May 1986, he was called to the Bar of New South Wales and practised as a barrister in the Criminal Division of the superior courts of Queensland as counsel for the defence.

John Oxley Library, State Library of Queensland

ABBREVIATIONS

GG Government Gazette

LA Legislative Assembly

LC Legislative Council

QPG Queensland Police Gazette

QSA Queensland State Archives

TSI Torres Strait Islanders

V & P Votes and Proceedings

CONTENTS

Preface 7

Introduction 9

Chapter 1 31

Chapter 2 125

Bibliography 159

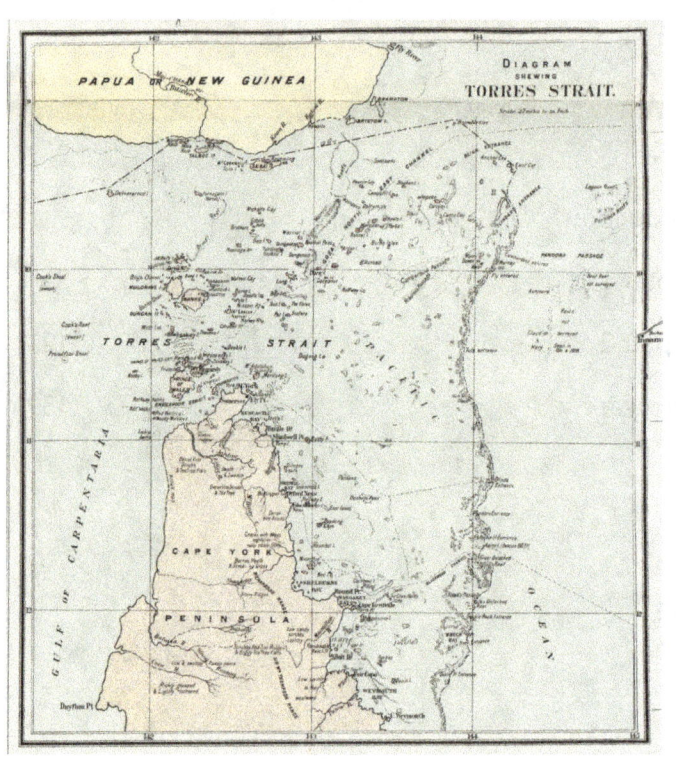

PREFACE

I began with the idea that I would write a complete history of marine incidents in Queensland waters and adjacent islands which involved indigenous elements. When first looked at, this seemed straightforward enough. After all, everyone is now writing about Aboriginals and their connection with this or that. It's the hip thing to do. So, linking Aboriginals to marine incidents in Queensland waters would be just another doddle. Noel Loos looked at something similar way back in the 1970s. The further I researched the issue the greater the complexity of the matter became.

Generally speaking, if one looks at Australian colonial history from a race perspective one could pose the following question:

Compare and contrast the treatment of Aboriginals and Chinese in each of the colonies of New South Wales, Victoria, Tasmania, South Australia, and West Australia.

This would be a valid exercise as each colony began with an indigenous population and most colonies were overrun by the Chinese pre-federation. However, when the colony of Queensland is examined, it might be noted that Queensland not only dealt with Aboriginals and Chinese on the mainland of the colony but also imported Pacific Islanders on work permits; expanded its colonial borders to include another aboriginal group called Torres Strait Islanders, and further still annexed part of an adjacent country, ultimately known as British New Guinea and involved itself in the administration of this group of people. As a consequence, the work became far too extensive to try and reduce to a book of even 500 pages.

Consequently, I divided the project into three areas of study: mainland indigenous natives and Torres Strait islanders, Papuans, and Pacific Islanders.[1] The research involving the first group produced an extensive range of data that revealed 95 marine incidents involving Australian and Torres Strait indigenous elements.

When this data was collected, sorted, classified, and the case studies written up together with the narrative and the conclusions, the study produced a manuscript of 103,600 words. This document was privately published for a limited academic audience, *Bêche-de-mer and the Binghis*.

The second area of study, marine incidents in Queensland waters and adjacent islands involving Papuan elements, again produced an impressive collection of data which when refined and analysed resulted in an equally extensive manuscript of 115,000 words which has also been published under the title of *Dispela Kantri Bilong Mi, Nau! Queensland Annexes New Guinea*.

The third area of study, marine incidents in Queensland waters and adjacent islands involving Pacific Islander elements, is still under study.

The following pages of this book represent an abridged and revised edition of the original manuscript without the inclusion of individual case studies.

---

[1] Indigenous means for these purposes any aboriginal native of Australia, Torres Strait, Papua, New Guinea, Pacific Islands & South Sea Islands; commonly known as Aborigines, Torres Strait Islanders, Papuans, Kanakas, Polynesians & South Sea Islanders.

INTRODUCTION

This book is about marine incidents occurring on or near Queensland waters and seaways from 1859 to Federation.[2] For the sake of clarity, I define a marine incident as follows:

> The death of or injury to officers and/or crew and/or passengers of a vessel;
> The loss of or damage to a vessel and/or the cargo; and/or
> A breach of Admiralty or Maritime legislation.[3]

Given the title of this book, that should suggest I will not be covering all the marine incidents that have occurred in the course of the settlement of Queensland. The incidents portrayed in this narrative have an element of indigenous participation.[4]

It is said that up until the time of W.E.H. Stanner, historians rarely if ever mentioned or portrayed Australian Aborigines

---

[2] On Federation, the Queensland border in the Torres Strait effectively became the Australian border.
[3] See the Australian Maritime Safety Authority for a comprehensive definition of a marine incident.
[4] Indigenous means for these purposes any aboriginal native of Australia, or Torres Strait.

in Australian colonial history. Stanner referred to this period of academic inattention to Australia's Aborigines, as 'the great Australian silence'. So, on the strength of that statement, I am about to attempt something novel by identifying those marine incidents in the colonial history of Queensland that involved the interaction of indigenous elements with the white maritime heritage of Queensland.

In identifying such incidents, I will endeavour to describe them in detail from original eye witness accounts or sources. Regrettably, these sources will be European as there are no indigenous sources.[5]

However, in the twenty-first century, commentators writing about Queensland's colonial history involving indigenous elements not only identify their contribution but also describe it in a way that suggests that Aboriginals were not passive victims but principal players driving the narrative and, in fact, pursuing particular lines of policy in response to white settler encroachment, even warfare.[6] In attempting to identify these particular types of marine incidents, it also appears that I am required to attribute a motive to the actions of the indigenous natives. Perhaps I can attempt to address that question in the concluding chapter of this book.

If the reader might peruse *Triumph in the Tropics* by R. Cilento

---

[5] This is a slightly contentious statement to make for some commentators will argue that in these circumstances the historian is required to interrogate and decode colonialist historical narratives in favour of the indigenes.

[6] See the works of Henry Reynolds.

and Clem Luck[7] the reader will observe that the authors adopted a view that the settlement of the Queensland colony was by way of opening up frontiers of interest or exploitation like Aborigines, forests, marine, pastoral, mining, and others. Consequently, they devoted a chapter to each area of activity.

In April 1976, Noel Loos completed a Ph.D. thesis, at James Cook University entitled *Aboriginal-European relations in North Queensland, 1861-1897*. He identified four frontiers of contact as follows:

> The pastoral, mining, farming, and fishing industries created frontiers of contact. The nature of each industry and the environment in which it occurred provided varying challenges to and allowed differing responses from the Aborigines, such that Aboriginal resistance on the mining, farming, and fishing frontiers indicated the inadequacy of Queensland's frontier policy which had evolved to meet the needs of rapid pastoral expansion.[8]

The question is how and in what way have indigenous elements crossed or intersected the maritime jurisdiction and who were these indigenous elements and what was the manner and method (form) of this interaction as to time, place, or other circumstances attending the incident; what were the manner and evidence of the indigenous contact?

---

[7] *Triumph in the tropics: an historical sketch of Queensland*/compiled and edited by Sir Raphael Cilento; with the assistance of Clem Lack; for the Historical Committee of the Centenary Celebrations Council of Queensland, Brisbane, Qld.: Smith & Paterson, 1959.

[8] Loos, Noel (1976) Aboriginal-European relations in North Queensland, 1861-1897. PhD thesis, James Cook University, p i.

MORETON BAY FREE SETTLEMENT

WHEREAS, ... the said District of Moreton Bay is no longer to be considered as a Penal Settlement; and that from and after the date hereof, all Settlers and other Free Persons shall be at liberty to proceed thither in like manner as to any other part of the Colony. This tenth day of February, one thousand eight hundred and forty-two. L. S. (Signed) George Gipps. By His Excellency's Command, E. Deas Thomson.[9]

By the time of separation, 1859, the settlement possessed more sheep, cattle, horses, and houses than it did in the previous seventeen years; but in what respect was the district more independent of extraneous aid than in 1842? Its ports, roads, and harbours were in a state of nature. Its streets were unformed and dangerous. Its banks and assurance offices were exotics; no steam companies were established; and the final settlements of all monetary transactions connected with the great pastoral interests of the district were affected in Sydney. It had to create direct trade and improve its ports and harbours, as well as the navigation of its rivers, all of which were undeveloped. The same thing may be said as to the means of communication with the interior, railroads had to be built as soon as possible. The establishment of telegraphic communication also had to be erected within the colony and with other colonies as well as the outside world of India and Europe.

Steamers ran daily on the river between Brisbane and Ipswich, and there was a fortnightly communication by steam with the ports of Maryborough, Gladstone, and Rockhampton. There was also weekly passage by steam packet with Sydney, the

---

[9] New South Wales Government Gazette 15 February 1842 [Issue No.13] p 267.

Introduction

voyage occupying from two to three days. Passage could also be had in coasters. With the movement of explorers, prospectors and settlers steadily northward, settlement, development, and supplies depended entirely on sea communications. Vessels sailed up the coast carrying supplies for the overland travellers: some prospectors and others took passage by sea rather than face the land journey. Both passengers and cargo had to be put ashore safely at a point on the coast nearest to their destination in sheltered water. As settlements grew and developed, merchant ships, in addition to maintaining services on the coast, carried Queensland products to overseas markets, returning with migrants and goods.

All well and good you may say, but what were the sailing directions or routes to be taken to reach these overseas markets? There were two routes, one by the south through Bass Strait, round Cape Leeuwin, and then onto Singapore or Port de Galle. The other was by the north, through the Torres Strait, and then onto Singapore or Port de Galle.[10] For example, when the 17th Regiment of Foot departed Australia for Madras, after seeing colonial service at Moreton Bay and New South Wales, one detachment sailed in the *Recovery* which left Sydney three months before the *Waterloo* left with the remainder. However, the *Recovery* only arrived nine days ahead of the *Waterloo*. After getting to the entrance of Bass Strait, the *Recovery* had to put back and re-pass Sydney Heads, taking the Torres Strait route. The *Waterloo* had a beautiful run of only six weeks.[11]

From Brisbane by the Torres Strait route, it was only seventeen days' distance from Galle, thus getting a gain of eight days

---
[10] There were two routes, an Inner and Outer. This work will be predominately concerned with the Inner route.
[11] *Sydney Monitor and Commercial Advertiser* 19 December 1838 p 2.

on each passage. Therefore, it was obvious that Queensland would strive to open its communication to the northward, as soon as ever it was in a position to afford it. There were some peculiarities about the Torres Strait route which tended to diminish its cost. The seas were generally tranquil, and vessels of much smaller size, and less expensive to work, could be relied upon to guarantee punctuality. The roughest part of the whole passage was between Sydney and Moreton Bay.[12]

GEOGRAPHICAL BOUNDARIES AND MARITIME JURISDICTION.

There is one other dimension to this study and that is the matter of the geographical boundaries of the colony of Queensland or to put it another way, the territorial and marine jurisdiction of Queensland. Letters Patent erecting Moreton Bay into a Colony, under the name of Queensland, and separated from the colony of New South Wales provided:

> so much of the said colony of New South Wales as lies northward of a line commencing on the sea coast at Point Danger, in latitude about 28 degrees 8 minutes south, and following the range thence which divides the waters of the Tweed, Richmond, and Clarence Rivers from those of the Logan and Brisbane Rivers, westerly, to the great dividing range between the waters falling to the east coast and those of the River Murray; following the great dividing range southerly to the range dividing the waters of Tenterfield Creek from those of the main head of the Dumaresq River; following that range

---

[12] *North Australian,* Ipswich and *General Advertiser* 10 July 1860 p 4 & *Brisbane Courier* 2 April 1875 p 3 The Torres Straits Route.

westerly to the Dumaresq River; and following that river (which is locally known as the Severn) downward to its confluence with the Macintyre River; thence following the Macintyre River, which lower down becomes the Barwan, downward to the 29th parallel of south latitude, and following that parallel westerly to the 141st meridian of east longitude, which is the eastern boundary of South Australia, together with all and every the adjacent Islands, their members and appurtenances, in the Pacific Ocean: And do by these presents separate from our said Colony of New South Wales and erect the said territory so described into a separate Colony to be called the Colony of Queensland.[13]

Unlike the other colonies, Queensland's boundaries were altered several times prior to Federation. At the time of separation from New South Wales in 1859, Queensland's western boundary was the same as the eastern boundary of South Australia, the 141st meridian of east longitude. Then on 12 April 1862, the western boundary of Queensland was moved further west to the 138th meridian of east longitude, together with all and every adjacent islands their members, and appurtenances in the Gulf of Carpentaria.[14] This extension of the boundary westward gave Queensland greater access to the Gulf including the Wellesley Islands and Burketown.

To mitigate the risk associated with navigating the Great Barrier Reef and Torres Strait, the settlement of Somerset, Cape York, was founded in September 1864, at the instigation of the Imperial authorities, as a station and harbour of refuge

---

[13] GG No. 1] 10 December 1859, p 1.
[14] GG Vol. III.] 23 June 1862 [No. 51 pp 295-296. The boundary effectively encroached upon the Northern Territory leaving the South Australian boundary intact.

for seamen wrecked on the reef or in the Straits. Somerset was also made a free port, in the hope of establishing a second Singapore.

Then in December 1871, the premier, Arthur Palmer, presented to Governor Normanby, a request to be forwarded to the Secretary of State for the Colonies for "Letters Patent conferring on the Government of Queensland territorial jurisdiction over all the Islands along the coast of the Colony within a distance of sixty miles therefrom". The Imperial government willingly granted the request. On 24 August 1872, the new frontier was established 60 miles from the coast. It was an arbitrary line drawn on an Admiralty chart.[15]

The settlement at Somerset with the port named Albany was maintained at the joint expense of the Imperial and colonial governments, but it failed to attract settlers, and when trade began to flow through Torres Strait, Somerset failed to derive benefit from it, for few vessels made it a port of call. On inquiry, it was discovered that the site was unsuitable; and, if Queensland desired to see a flourishing settlement, commanding the trade of the northern coast waters, a more advantageous site had to be selected. Captain Moresby of H.M.S. *Basilisk*, searched on Imperial account and recommended the northern portion of Hammond Island, one of the Prince of Wales group. Messrs. Jardine, Dalrymple, and Aplin, after examination, also pointed out suitable sites. Mr. Dalrymple recommended the south-west end of Hammond Island, Mr. Jardine the south-west end of Friday Island, and Mr. Aplin the north-west end of Thursday Island. In this dilemma, the colonial government dispatched Commander Heath, R.N., to make an examination and report.

---

[15] GG Vol. XIII.] 17 August 1872 [No. 80 pp 1269-1271 & Vol. XIII.] 24 August 1872 [No. 87 p 1325.

This officer left Brisbane on 23 April 1875, and after serious investigations, recommended Vivien Point, the south-western extremity of Thursday Island.[16]

In early 1876 a cabinet decision was made to move the Somerset establishment to Thursday Island. Mr. Robert Muter Stewart, Colonial Secretary moved the vote for the Somerset Harbour of Refuge during the 1876 debate on Supply. In doing so, he said that the settlement was in the course of removal to Thursday Island; vote agreed to and passed.[17] In response to the vote for the Harbour of Refuge, Mr. W. H. Walsh, Warrego, drew a picture of Thursday Island, as an "important British possession," defended by eight native troopers, aboriginals, and, eloquently remarked, "Are we, Sir, as Englishmen, become so debased, have we sunk so low, Sir, that we must rest our defence on eight aboriginals, &c., &c."[18]

Thursday Island is one of many islands in the Torres Strait. It is close to the Prince of Wales, Horn, Hammond, Friday, Wednesday, and Goode Islands, and is centrally situated and not more than one or two miles from each of the islands above mentioned. It was admirably suited for the purpose, being in the track of all vessels sailing through the Inner Channel, as well as all vessels taking the Outer Route, by the Great North East Channel, near the coast of New Guinea. The settlement on Thursday Island was such that no matter which route ships took through Torres Strait, they must pass within a few miles of the new port. Thursday Island was so situated that, vessels to or from the north must pass close into Goode Island, upon which island the colony had erected a signal mast to signalise

---

[16] *Rockhampton Bulletin* 5 July 1875 p 2.
[17] *Queenslander* 14 October 1876 p 8.
[18] *Maryborough Chronicle, Wide Bay and Burnett Advertiser* 19 October 1876 p 2.

all vessels and report or signal the same on to Thursday Island. On or about 20 July 1877, Henry Marjoribanks Chester was appointed Sub-Collector of Customs and Harbour Master at Thursday Island; and Police Magistrate at Thursday Island.[19]

The Western Pacific High Commission was established by the British Government by an Order in Council in 1877 to extend British authority over British subjects in the islands of the southwest Pacific, then outside any formal colonial control.

BRITISH ORDER IN COUNCIL, for the Regulation of British jurisdiction in the Western Pacific Islands (Friendly Islands, Navigators' Islands, Union Islands, Phœnix Islands, Ellice Islands, Gilbert Islands, Marshall Islands or Archipelago, Caroline Islands, Solomon Islands, Santa Cruz Islands, Rotumah Island, part of Island of New Guinea, Islands or Archipelago of New Britain and New Ireland, Louisiade Archipelago, &c.) and the water within 3 miles of every island or place above-mentioned. Dated at Osborne, August 13, 1877.[20]

Rising out of this extension of British control of the Western Pacific, on 22 March 1878, Arthur Gordon, High Commissioner for the Western Pacific appointed Henry M. Chester to be Judicial Commissioner in and for the Murray and Darnley Islands, Western Pacific Ocean.[21]

With the new arrangements implemented in the Torres Strait and the ever-increasing trade and traffic through and within the Straits, it was considered politically expedient to move

---

[19] GG Vol. XXI.] 21 July 1877 [No. 17 pp 154-155.
[20] This was an order formally made in the name of the Queen by the Privy Council having the same force in law as legislation. The Order is in fact an extensive piece of legislation.
[21] GG Vol. XXII.] 23 March 1878. [No. 41 p 753.

the border once again.[22] To that end, Queen Victoria issued Letters Patent to obtain rectification of the maritime boundary of Queensland, to include certain islands in Torres Strait at present beyond the jurisdiction of the colony. Accordingly, the Queensland Coast Islands Act of 1879 was enacted to annex the following:

> Certain Islands in Torres Straits and lying between the Continent of Australia and the Island of New Guinea that is to say all Islands included within a line drawn from Sandy Cape northward to the south-eastern limit of Great Barrier Reefs thence following the line of the Great Barrier Reefs to their north-eastern extremity, near the latitude of nine and a half degrees south, thence in a north-westerly direction, embracing East, Anchor and Bramble Cays thence from Bramble Cays in a line west by south (south seventy-nine degrees west) true; embracing Warrior Reef, Saibai and Tuan Islands, thence diverging in a north-westerly direction so as to embrace the group known as the Talbot Islands; thence to and embracing the Deliverance Islands and onwards in a west by south direction (true) to the meridian of one hundred and thirty-eight degrees of east longitude.[23]

Cooktown, 13 April 1883. The Government schooner *Pearl* arrived from New Guinea, with Mr. Chester, the Police Magistrate at Thursday Island, who brought news that he took formal possession of New Guinea, in the name of the Queensland Government, by proclamation read at Port

---

[22] Mullins, SP, 'Queensland's Quest for Torres Strait: the delusion of inevitability', *Journal of Pacific History*, vol. 27, no. 2, 1992, pp 165-180.
[23] Supplement to the Queensland Government Gazette of Saturday, 21st June, 1879 No. 108 p 1379 & GG Vol. XXV.] 21 July 1879 [No.10 p 143. See map at p 29 below.

Moresby on 4 April 1883:[24]

I, Henry, Marjoribanks Chester, resident magistrate at Thursday Island, in the Colony of Queensland, acting under instructions from the Government of the said colony, do hereby take possession of all that portion of New Guinea and the islands and inlets adjacent thereto, lying between the 141st and 155th meridians of east longitude, in the name and on behalf of Her Most Gracious Majesty Queen Victoria, her heirs, and successors. In token whereof, I have hoisted and saluted the British flag at Port Moresby in New Guinea this fourth day of April, in the year of our Lord one thousand eight hundred and eighty-three. God Save the Queen! (Signed) Henry M. Chester.[25]

Ministerial Statement. The Premier (Sir T. McIlwraith) said:

> I received a telegram from the Agent-General in London. The telegram read as follows:
>
> June 3rd, 1883. Lord Derby in House last night disallowed annexation. States the other Powers making settlement would not be viewed as friendly act. Prepared to extend to New Guinea the power of High Commissioner. Unable to obtain interview today.

I do not wish to comment on the reasons given by either the Secretary of State for the Colonies or by the Premier of Great Britain, for the course so inimical to the interests of Queensland and the other Australian colonies which the mother country has thought fit to adopt on the present occasion. I merely wish to

---

[24] *Telegraph* 14 April 1883 p 4.
[25] *Telegraph* 23 April 1883 p 2.

point out that so far as Queensland is concerned and the other colonies, too, I look upon the act of annexation of New Guinea to British territory or, at all events, to Queensland territory, as an accomplished fact. I question, and with all modesty I do it, I question the legality of the decision of Mr. Gladstone when he says that our action was null and void.[26]

However, the UK government subsequently offered to establish a coastal protectorate, the cost of which, the colonies would contribute. At the Inter-Colonial Convention of 1883, held at Sydney, the colonies approved the annexation of New Guinea, and an agreement was quickly reached. It was a question of the extent of the protectorate, and it appeared that at the last meeting before the autumn recess, the British Cabinet had at one moment agreed to proclaim a protectorate over the whole of non-Dutch New Guinea, or all save the stretch of northern coast between 141^0 and 145^0 east longitude. It was at this stage that the Government got its first definite inkling of the intentions of Germany.

Sometime later, an impression arose within the Australian colonies that the British Government together with the Governments of Germany and France had colluded for a mutual division of the unappropriated islands of the Pacific as a way of solving the Pacific question. Two German war ships *Elizabeth* and *Hyäne*, arrived in New Guinea under instructions from the German Imperial authorities and established a protectorate on the north coast of New Guinea; the German flag was formerly hoisted and saluted on 4 November 1884. The same ceremony was performed by those vessels at New Britain, New Ireland, New Hanover, Duke of York, Admiralty, and D'Entrecasteaux Islands. A German steamer also visited various portions of the

---

[26] Hansard, LA, 4 July 1883 p 89-90, abridged.

north coast of New Guinea, and adjoining islands, to conclude treaties with the natives for the transfer of land to the German Government so that the latter could establish German claims to territory in Northern New Guinea and the neighbouring islands in preference to any other nation.[27]

BRITISH PROTECTORATE OF NEW GUINEA.

The British Government, on receiving an assurance from the Australian colonies that they would contribute £15,000 per annum towards the costs of the New Guinea jurisdiction, agreed to establish a protectorate over New Guinea and the adjacent islands.[28] London, 9 October 1884. The Imperial Government ordered Commodore Erskine to proclaim a British protectorate over the south Coast of New Guinea and the islands immediately adjacent.[29] At Port Moresby, on the sixth day of November 1884, by proclamation, Commodore Erskine of the Australian Station established a British Protectorate over the territories named in the schedule:

Schedule.

All that portion of the southern shores of New Guinea, commencing from the boundary of that portion of the country claimed by the Government of the Netherlands on the 141st meridian of east longitude to East Cape, with all islands adjacent thereto south of East Cape to Kosman

---

27 *Sydney Morning Herald* 20 December 1884 p 14 & Singleton Argus 20 December 1884 p 2.
28 The New Guinea and Pacific Jurisdiction Contribution Act of 1884, 48 Vic. No. 7; Supplement to the Queensland Government Gazette, 28 August 1884, No. 34, p 743.
29 *Daily Telegraph* 11 October 1884 p 5.

Island inclusive, together with the islands in the Goschen Straits, and also the D'Entrecasteaux Group, and smaller islands adjacent. Given on board Her Majesty's ship *Nelson* at the harbour of Port Moresby, on the 6th day of November 1884. (Signed) James Elphinstone Erskine, Commodore. God Save the Queen.[30]

His Excellency the Governor received the following message from Cooktown: H.M.S. *Swinger* arrived from New Guinea this a.m. Protectorate proclaimed 6 November 1884; five warships present; fifty native chiefs; ceremony very impressive.[31] Major-General Sir Peter Scratchley, R.E. was appointed by the Imperial Government Special Commissioner for New Guinea and the adjacent islands in the Protectorate together with Mr. Romilly.[32]

It seemed that the spheres of action between Germany and Great Britain in New Guinea required clarification resulting in the following treaty:

> Letter from Earl Granville, Foreign Office, April 25, 1885 to Count Münster:
>
> Proposes boundary between British and German Protectorate as follows: Starting from the coast near Mitre Rock on the 8th parallel of south latitude, it would follow that parallel until it is intersected by the meridian of 147° east longitude: would proceed thence in a straight line in a north-westerly direction to the point of intersection of

---

30 *Telegraph* 19 November 1884 p 2; GG Vol. XXXV.] 23 December 1884 [No.113, p 2037 & GG Vol. XXXVI.] 7 March 1885 [No. 42, p 902.
31 *Brisbane Courier* 15 November 1884 p 5 & 17 December 1884 p 5; *Telegraph* 19 November 1884 p 2 & *Queensland Times, Ipswich Herald and General Advertiser* 15 November 1884 p 5.
32 *Sydney Morning Herald* 5 January 1885 p 8.

the 6th parallel of south latitude, with the 144th meridian of east longitude, and would continue thence in a west-north-westerly direction until it meets the point of intersection of the 5th parallel of south latitude with the 141st meridian of east longitude."

Letter from Count Münster, German Embassy, London, April 29, 1885 to Earl Granville: Accepts proposed boundary.[33]

On the death of Scratchley, the hon. John Douglas was appointed Special Commissioner for the British Protectorate of New Guinea with effect 26 December 1885.[34] Then on 4 September 1888, the British Protectorate of New Guinea was erected into the Crown colony of British New Guinea with William Macgregor appointed as administrator. The colony was subject to the instructions of Queensland; see the British New Guinea Order in Council of 1888, in particular, the British New Guinea (Queensland) Act of 1887.[35] Externally, the most important political event was the final settlement in 1895 of the boundary with Dutch New Guinea. The frontier was fixed 1½ miles east of the 141st east meridian, as far as the Fly River, which it follows between the two points where the river crosses the meridian, so that divided jurisdiction over the river might be avoided; it then follows the meridian to the point of intersection of the then German, Dutch and British possessions.

---

[33] British New Guinea (Papua), Foreign Office Handbook No. 88, H.M. Stationery Office, London, 1920 p 61.
[34] GG Vol. XXXVIII.] 22 March 1886 [No. 38, p 1105.
[35] GG Vol. XLV.] 11 September 1888 [No. 9, pp 121-133.

RELEVANT LEGISLATION

Aboriginals

An Act to Prevent the Improper Employment of Aboriginal Natives of Australia and New Guinea on Ships in Queensland Waters.[36] Assented to 17 November 1884. Short Title: The Native Labourers' Protection Act of 1884. 48 Vic. No. 20.

An Act to make Provision for the better Protection and Care of the Aboriginal and Half-caste Inhabitants of the Colony, and to make more effectual Provision for Restricting the Sale and Distribution of Opium.[37] Assented to 15 December 1897. Short Title: Aboriginals Protection and Restriction of the Sale of Opium Act, 1897. 61 Vic. No. 17.

Regulations under the Aboriginals Protection and Restriction of the Sale of Opium Act, 1897.[38]

An Act to Amend "The Aboriginals Protection and Restriction of the Sale of Opium Act, 1897," and for other purposes. [Reserved: His Majesty's Assent Proclaimed, 3 May 1902.] Short Title: The Aboriginals Protection and Restriction of the Sale of Opium Act, 1901.

Pearl-shell and Bêche-de-mer Fishery

An Act to Regulate the Pearl-shell and Bêche-de-mer Fishery in the Colony of Queensland.[39] Assented to 15 September 1881.

---

[36] Supplement to the Queensland Government Gazette, 20 November 1884, No. 93, p 1737.
[37] Supplement to the Queensland Government Gazette, 16 December 1897 No. 146 p 1387.
[38] GG Vol. LXXII.] 23 September 1899. [No. 87 p746-747.
[39] Supplement to the Queensland Government Gazette, 17 September 1881 No. 38 p 659.

This Act shall commence and take effect from 1 January 1882.

Short Title: Pearl-shell and Bêche-de-mer Fishery Act of 1881. 45 Vic. No. 2.

An Act to Amend The Pearl-shell and Bêche-de-mer Fishery Act of 1881.[40] Assented to 4 September 1886.

Short Title: Pearl-shell and Bêche-de-mer Fishery Act Amendment Act of 1886. 50 Vic. No. 2.

An Act to further Amend The Pearl-Shell and Bêche-de-mer Fishery Act of 1881.[41] Assented to 13 November 1891.

Short Title: The Pearl-Shell and Bêche-de-mer Fishery Act Amendment Act of 1891. 55° Vict. No. 29.

An Act to Amend The Pearl-shell and Bêche-de-mer Fishery Act Amendment Act of 1881.[42] Assented to 29 August 1893.

Short Title: Pearl-shell and Bêche-de-mer Fishery Act Amendment Act of 1893. 57 Vic. No. 7.

An Act to further Amend The Pearl-shell and Bêche-de-mer Fishery Act Amendment Act of 1891.[43] Assented to 21 December 1896.

Short Title: Pearl-shell and Bêche-de-mer Fishery Act Amendment Act of 1896. 60 Vic. No. 32.

---

[40] Supplement to the Queensland Government Gazette, 10 September 1886 No. 43 p 951.
[41] Supplement to the Queensland Government Gazette, 16 November 1891 No. 82 p 915.
[42] Supplement to the Queensland Government Gazette, 30 August 1893 No. 124 p 1059.
[43] Supplement to the Queensland Government Gazette, 23 December 1896 No. 170 p 1488.

An Act to Amend the Pearl-shell and Bêche-de-mer Fishery Acts.[44] Reserved: Her Majesty's assent proclaimed 25 August 1899.

Short Title: The Pearl-shell and Bêche-de-mer Fishery Act of 1898. 63 Vic. No. 3.

An Act to regulate the Pearl-shell and Bêche-de-mer Fisheries in Australasian Waters adjacent to the Colony of Queensland. Reserved 20 January 1888. Queen's assent proclaimed, 19 July 1888. 51 Vic. No. 1.[45]

An Act to regulate the Pearl Shell and Bêche-de-mer Fisheries in Australasian Waters adjacent to the Colony of Queensland.

[Reserved 20 January 1888. Queen's Assent Proclaimed 19 July 1888.]

Whereas by certain Acts of the Parliament of the Colony of Queensland provision has been made for regulating the Pearl Shell and Bêche-de-mer Fisheries in the territorial waters of that Colony: And whereas, by reason of the geographical position of many of the Islands forming portion of that Colony, vessels employed in such Fisheries are, in the prosecution of their business, sometimes within and sometimes beyond the territorial jurisdiction of Queensland: And whereas it is expedient that the provisions of the said Acts should extend and apply to such vessels during all the time during which they are so employed, and that for that purpose the provisions of the said Acts, so far as they are applicable to extra-territorial waters, should be extended to such waters by an Act of the

---

[44] GG Vol. LXXII.] 25 August 1899 [No. 59 p 507 & Supplement to the Queensland Government Gazette, 29 August 1899 No. 65 p 549.
[45] GG Vol. XLIV.] 24 August 1888 [No. 94, p 1237 & GG Vol. XLIX.] 1 February 1890 [No. 23 p 367.

Federal Council of Australasia: Be it therefore enacted by the Queen's Most Excellent Majesty, by and with the advice and consent of the Federal Council of Australasia, assembled at Hobart, in the Colony of Tasmania, and by the authority of the same, as follows:

This Act may be cited as "The Queensland Pearl Shell and Bêche-de-mer Fisheries (Extra-territorial) Act of 1888," and shall commence and take effect on and from the date of Her Majesty's assent thereto being proclaimed in Queensland.[46]

---

[46] GG VOL. XLIV.] 24 August 1888. [No. 94 p 1238.

Introduction

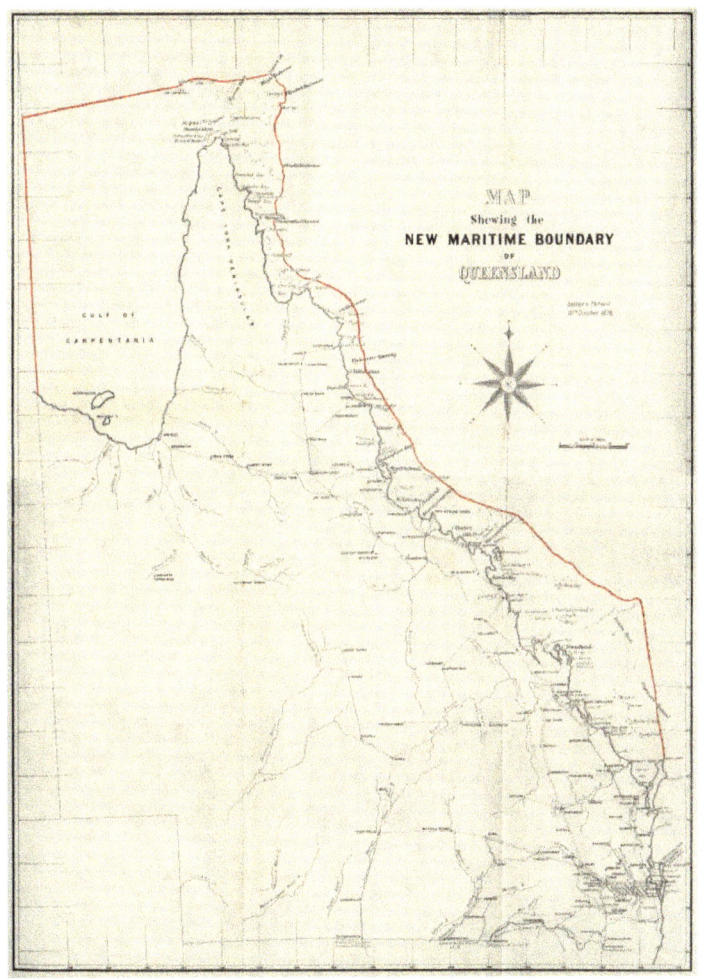

New Maritime Boundary of Queensland — Letters Patent, 10 October 1878, http://nla.gov.au/nla.obj-232289317 and Queensland Coast Islands Act of 1879.

1

The Bêche-de-mer Industry in Queensland

The Bêche-de-mer industry has been described by some as Queensland's oldest, quaintest, and most colourful industry, which in its heyday yielded several million pounds of revenue. For the speculator who wished to enter the industry in colonial times, the main difficulty confronting him was the attitude of the Binghis. It was well known that the natives along the coast of the Great Barrier Reef were about the most treacherous in Queensland, and many murders of white men were due to them. It was also affirmed by those in a position to know that the Aboriginals indulged in cannibalism. With such material from which to recruit labour, the industry promised to be a hazardous one; but, with perseverance and courage, some of the natives became expert in the work. The outstanding feature of the industry was how the masters of the vessels were able to gain the confidence and control of their dusky workmen and women. Therein lies the rub.

Bêche-de-mer fishing is often quoted in the same context as pearl-shell fishing as if there was little difference between the two. It has been said that the bêche-de-mer industry was "boxed" with pearl-shelling in an endeavour to extract revenue from New South Wales capitalists who were fishing in Queensland waters; the Government, unfortunately, placed disabilities upon bêche-de-mer fishing, which was an entirely local industry, and which, but for the taxation imposed, might have been largely extended and have contributed materially to the prosperity of Northern Queensland.[47] However, the major difference is that very few, if any, Aboriginals were employed in the pearlshell industry. Perhaps the following quote will suffice to explain why:

> Mainland aborigines are not employed to any extent in the pearlshell industry, as they are not reliable enough to act as tenders to divers or as pump hands and are useless as dress-divers; but two or three owners of small boats employ a small number of them as what are called 'swimming divers' in shallow water. These are mostly well-treated and are regularly shipped on proper articles and duly paid off at the Thursday Island Shipping Office.[48]

Bêche-de-mer is a sea animal also known as a sea cucumber (Holothuroidea) which was and still is, used to make soup, which is consumed chiefly in China. In Indonesian culture, it is known as trepang, and fishing for trepang is known as trepaning, which was carried out in Arnhem Land by

---

[47] *Queensland Figaro* 12 July 1884 p 12.
[48] Qld Parl. 1897 V & P Vol. II p 23ff.

Makassans and Aborigines for a very long time. However, Makassan trepaning is not of interest in this study. Nor is the complete history of bêche-de-mer fishing in Australian waters. It had long been known that the reefs of Torres Strait and the N. E. coast of Queensland produced in abundance bêche-de-mer. Newspaper records suggest that bêche-de-mer was imported into Sydney from North Queensland and the South Pacific from about 1850 onwards. The *Sydney Morning Herald* reported as follows:

> Maryborough, March 5, 1850. Captain Cooper, of the *Beaver*, while at anchor close to Fraser's Island, procured five or six bêche-de-mer, which he pronounced a very fair sample. Captain Cooper seems quite confident that large quantities of this sea-slug may be found all along the coast to the north of Wide Bay. Captain Cooper supposes the discovery will be of immense importance to this colony (NSW), more particularly at present for unless the British Government take speedy and decisive measures to give protection to British subjects carrying on bêche-de-mer fisheries on the South Sea Islands, that trade must be abandoned. First-rate stations can be formed along this coast for carrying on bêche-de-mer fisheries, and the natives for a little flour and tobacco could be got to render the most valuable assistance to such establishments, and when not required easily kept at a safe distance through their awful dread of firearms. I trust some of the Sydney capitalists will turn their attention to this important subject.[49]

During the 1860s, bêche-de-mer appeared to become a valuable trading commodity at Sydney. The following is from

---

[49] *Sydney Morning Herald* 19 March 1850 p 3, abridged.

the *Sydney Morning Herald*:

> IMPORTS. February 2, 1867.
>
> *Boomerang* (s), from Cleveland Bay 18 bales wool, O. B. Ebsworth; 20 tierces tallow, 121 bags bêche-de-mer, R Towns and Co.
>
> *Woodlark*, from Torres Strait 18 tons bêche-de-mer, R Towns and Co.
>
> *Kate Kearney*, from South Sea Islands 40 tons sulphur, 6 tuns coconut oil, 5 tuns black oil, 14 cwt bêche-de-mer, H. Burnes.[50]

R Towns & Co, in 1854, secured a foothold in Brisbane when they bought the Commercial Hotel, Wharf, and Store, in South Brisbane from Mr. McCabe for £3000.[51] Perhaps the first sign that R Towns & Co were trading in bêche-de-mer out of Brisbane was when the schooner *Uncle Tom* was towed down river to Lytton, by the *Premier*, s.s. She was bound for the South Sea Islands, to return the islanders imported in 1863 by Captain R. Towns, to their native places. After landing her passengers, the schooner cruised among the islands in search of bêche-de-mer, and then returned to Brisbane with those islanders who had signed a contract of labour.[52]

John Jardine in his report on the new settlement near Cape York of Somerset, on 1 March 1865, to the Colonial Secretary, Brisbane made the following observation:

---

[50] *Sydney Morning Herald* 4 February 1867 p 4.
[51] *Sydney Morning Herald* 14 February 1854 p 5.
[52] *Brisbane Courier* 13 September 1864 p 2.

23. The natives of the islands to the northward and eastward are said to be of milder disposition, especially the Darnley Islanders—of whom Captain Edwards, of Sydney, who had a "Bêche-de-mer" fishing establishment there during the last year, speaks in high terms as being of friendly dispositions ...[53]

Then from the *Brisbane Courier* of 6 December 1865, a further report by A. E. D., Barque *Caroline Elizabeth*, Port Albany, September 30:

> Since I have been here, I have had the pleasure of making the acquaintance of Captain Edwards, who, in connection with the firm of R. Towns and Co. has been collecting bêche-de-mer during the last four years. Captain Edwards has at present in his employ three vessels, and the nature of the trade he pursues has necessarily made him thoroughly acquainted with the prevailing weather and navigation of the localities he has visited.[54]

The following report in the *Queensland Times, Ipswich Herald and General Advertiser* of 12 January 1865 gave the first inkling of R. Towns & Co. taking an interest in the port of Cleveland Bay:

> ... which was sent to Sydney by Mr. Towns' ships, who, Mr. Black informs me, is going to make a depot of Cleveland Bay for his ships in the Pacific and China trade.[55]

---

[53] *Queensland Times, Ipswich Herald* and *General Advertiser* 24 June 1865 p 3.
[54] *Brisbane Courier* 6 December 1865 p 3
[55] Page 4.

Pursuant to the Sugar and Coffee Regulations, R. Towns made application for a lease of 1280 acres, near Cleveland Bay which was granted on 26 April 1865.[56]

The *Woodlark*, Captain Anderson, from the Coral Sea Fisheries anchored off Magnetical (sic, Magnetic) Island on 15 December 1866. She brought some twenty tons of bêche-de-mer, and the remainder of the cargo was shipped by the *Berengaria* direct to China. Some thirty or forty natives (kanakas) were also landed at Cleveland Bay, to be re-shipped on board the *Blue Bell*, engaged in the same trade. The *Woodlark* sailed on 21 December 1866 for Sydney direct.[57]

Port Denison, 6 October 1866. The *Percy* landed 50 kanakas for the bêche-de-mer trade.[58] Captain Croker reported a large whaleboat, in the charge of Captain Godfrey, passed through Hervey's Bay late March 1867 from Sydney, for the island of South St. Bernard's, Torres Strait, where she engaged in the bêche-de-mer trade. Besides the captain, there was only one other white man on board, the boat being manned by South Sea Islanders.[59]

Somerset, 6 September 1870. The schooner *Kate Kearney* was awaiting the arrival of her consorts, *Melanie*, and cutter *Fanny*. These vessels were well found in boats and men; and would search for pearl-shell in the Great Bight[60] and on the adjacent coasts, while the cutter will act as tender to them and cruise between Somerset and New Guinea. There were upwards of

---

[56] *Brisbane Courier* 8 July 1865 p 5.
[57] *Brisbane Courier* 14 January 1867 p 3 & *Sydney Morning Herald* 10 January 1867 p 4.
[58] *Brisbane Courier* 13 October 1866 p 6.
[59] *Maryborough Chronicle, Wide Bay* and *Burnett Advertiser* 6 April 1867 p 2; *Brisbane Courier* 20 April 1867 p 4.
[60] Gulf of Papua.

300 Polynesians employed by vessels pursuing bêche-de-mer fishing.[61]

John Jardine in a report from Somerset, 1 October 1871, to the Colonial Secretary made the following observation:

> The only new arrivals on the pearl banks that I know of (although I hear rumours of others, and Captain Bisset, of the *Restless*, reports many small craft fitting out in Sydney) are the *Australian Packet*, Captain Hovell, and schooner *Margaret and Jane*, Captain Tucker, making nine (9) vessels in all, employing upwards of two hundred (200) men. Captain Delargy, of the *Active*, reports having seventy tons (70) of bêche-de-mer, of the probable value of £7000; and also tells me that the master of the schooner *Matilda* has enticed away a number of the natives belonging to the *James Merriman* and that reprisals are meditated by Captain Williams. Further proof, if true, and if proof is still required, of the necessity for supervision. Of the pearl fisheries I have very little information but believe that none of the vessels are doing as well as hitherto.[62]

The introduction of the Kidnapping Act, 1872 by the Imperial Government, which took effect in Queensland from 31 August 1872,[63] put paid to the employment of kanakas in the bêche-de-mer industry as evidenced by the following:

> The Act was very properly passed to put a stop to outrages in the importation of labour to Fiji and Queensland. What we required was that vessels belonging to this

---

[61] *Maryborough Chronicle, Wide Bay* and *Burnett Advertiser* 22 October 1870 p 4 & *Empire* 8 August 1870 p 2.
[62] *Brisbane Courier* 21 November 1871 p 3.
[63] Qld GG Vol. XIII.] 31 August 1872 [No.97, p 1407. PACIFIC ISLANDERS' PROTECTION (UK). [35 AND 36 Vic.] [CH. 19.]

colony (NSW) should be allowed to take native crews from the islands for the purpose of carrying out pearl shell and bêche-de-mer fishing in Torres Straits and elsewhere, and we were prepared to point out how it could be done, and the rights of all parties maintained under the surveillance of the Government through her Majesty's ships. We requested that our petition might be forwarded to the Imperial Government, supported by the recommendation and approval of the Government of New South Wales.

Mr. Parkes (Colonial Secretary) said that he had watched the effect of the Kidnapping Act with a good deal of concern. He was aware of the importance of the trade to this colony, and he had every reason to believe that to a large extent that trade was carried on in a manner in every way creditable to those engaged in it. He had been aware that the operation of the Act had interfered with this trade, and he was quite sure that the Government would be glad to make any representations on this subject that would have the effect of relieving legitimate trade from any vexatious interference.[64]

This was confirmed by Captain J. Moresby of H.M.S. *Basilisk* when he reported in 1873 as follows:

Having made a tour of all the pearl-shelling and bêche-de-mer stations before sailing for New Guinea, on our return to Cape York I drew Mr. Jardine's attention to the fishery question. All fishing operations were now suspended till the receipt of government licences. The Polynesian islanders had been freed from their servitude

---

[64] *Sydney Morning Herald* 24 September 1874 p 2.

and sent to their homes, and the law had now provided such enactments as would secure righteous treatment for them in making a compact to serve their old masters again. The Torres Straits islanders entertained a perfectly friendly feeling towards the white men stationed on their islands and were willing and anxious to serve them for fair pay; whilst such service would be useful in civilising them.[65]

It cannot be stated categorically that no Aboriginals were employed in the bêche-de-mer industry before the Imperial Kidnapping Act, 1872. However, it needs to be remembered that the majority of bêche-de-mer boats in North Queensland operated out of Sydney and employed kanakas for bêche-de-mer fishing. From the limited descriptions of bêche-de-mer fishers set out above, it appears that in Queensland waters, a crew of South Sea Islanders was a prerequisite for the harvesting and preparation of the product for market.

Bêche-de-mer fishing might be described as follows:

> There are several kinds of sea slugs or bêche-de-mer, but the three principal kinds are "teat fish," "small black fish," and "small red fish," which are considered as representing first, second, and third qualities. When cured, "teat fish" takes from 8000 to 8700 to weigh a ton; this species is about 10in. in length and 12in. in circumference, black, smooth, and glossy, rounded on the back and sides, and flattened below with ten teat-like projections on each side. The "small red-fish" is considerably less in size; it takes about 18,600, when cured, to weigh a ton. The "small black fish" is still

---

[65] Surveys and Discoveries, &c., Captain Moresby, R.N. p 232.

smaller. The bêche-de-mer is collected on the reefs at low water, or when the depth is so trifling that it can be seen at the bottom, and be picked up by diving, and this is where the assistance of the blackfellows comes in. The gins are excellent collectors; hence the presence of so many in this industry. The headquarters or station is generally formed on some island. Large "pots"— generally the halves of ships' tanks--are set up in which to boil the fish. The contents of the pots are stirred with a pole, and the stomach, entrails, &c., which the fish throw out in abundance, are picked out from time to time and set aside. When they are judged to be sufficiently cooked, they are scooped out and thrown upon the sand, and the pot re-filled; and so on until all have been cooked. Then the "teat fish" are each slit along the belly with a knife, and usually, a short piece of stick is put into each, to keep the edges apart and to facilitate drying; but the small red fish are seldom opened. The next process is drying, and for this purpose, generally, "open batters" are considered sufficient; these are wooden platforms, about 5ft. high. The fish are then laid upon the batters in a single layer and are turned about twelve hours afterwards. Under the batters, enormous fires are kept burning day and night. At length, they are removed from the batters and finally sorted and bagged. From first picking it on the reef, until it is finally put away cured, each fish has probably been handled from six to twenty times, everything depending upon the amount of heat received and its regularity.[66]

The pay and conditions of the binghis were as follows:

---

[66] *Queensland Times, Ipswich Herald* and *General Advertiser* 22 November 1890 p 3, abridged.

All aborigines employed in the bêche-de-mer fisheries have to be brought to the nearest port for registration and discharge before the shipping master, and for which formality, in the former instance, a registration of 2s. 6d. per head is charged. The wages earned by these aborigines range from 5s. to 20s. per month, with all rations provided, 10s. representing the most customary one. These wages are invariably paid in kind, goods to the amount earned and consisting chiefly of clothing and tobacco, being usually selected. The lowest wage of 5s. per month is earned by the women, or "gins," who accompany the men engaged, and who at many of the curing-stations are employed mainly in cleaning and preparing the bêche-de-mer for the smokehouse.[67]

John Oxley Library, State Library of Queensland.
Binghis preparing Bêche-de-mer.

---

[67] Qld Parl. 1890 V & P Vol. III p 727ff; *Brisbane Courier* 15 December 1890 p 7 & *Queenslander* 27 December 1890 p 1226.

John Oxley Library, State Library of Queensland.

The above evidence suggests it was a hand-harvested fishery, with animals caught principally by wading and some diving. Based on the above description of the steps involved in catching, processing, and the quantity required, it would be fair to say that the industry was labour intensive involving high risk and hardship. Accordingly, there would be a high demand for unskilled or low-skilled labourers. To that end, bêche-de-mer fishers after 1872 began to employ aboriginal labour[68] for the collecting and processing of the sea slug as their labour was unregulated. The configuration of the employment appeared to be from twelve to fifteen Aboriginals, besides the master and a regular crew of four per vessel. The Aboriginals harvested the fish and assisted in preparing and curing the product.[69]

On 7 October 1874, the *Brisbane Courier* reported from Cooktown that Mr. George Williams, secured about five tons of bêche-de-mer, worth from £110 to £125 per ton, and that Captain Dear's bêche-de-mer fishery had collected, as much as half a ton at a day from the fishing grounds on Turtle Reef, a great portion being teat-fish, worth from £120 to £140 per ton.[70]

On 20 April 1875, Governor W. W. Cairns wrote to Lord Carnarvon enclosing a report on the pearl fisheries of Torres Strait by C. Aplin PM of Somerset, dated 3 March 1875 in which Cairns observed:

> It is noticeable and strange that but three small Queensland vessels are engaged in fishing for the pearl shell oyster, or bêche-de-mer, or in collecting tortoise

---

[68] It is not clear, but it may be that aboriginal includes Torres Strait Islander as well as mainland natives.
[69] A. O. Mackenzie before the Pearl-Shell and Bêche-de-mer Commission, Queensland, 1908 p 21.
[70] Page 2 of *Courier*.

shell as compared with the enterprise shown by the more distant colony of New South Wales.[71]

Aplin's report concentrated on the pearl shell fishery because according to him it generated in 1874, £27,840 worth of shell. On the other hand, bêche-de-mer generated 60 tons of product valued at £3,000. He listed 15 vessels of 1270 tons, 31 boats, and a total of 624 men all in the employ of New South Wales interests. And described the labour employed as nearly all mainland Aboriginals and the Torres Strait Islanders, who had good relations with their respective employers. He recommended that the government should derive revenue from the industry in support of the services the government provided in the Straits.[72]

Mr. McKinlay, of Edward-street, Brisbane, engaged, a short time ago, several newly arrived South Sea Islanders, to proceed to his fishing station in the Straits. Subsequently, he was informed that to remove the islanders beyond the soil of Queensland proper would be in violation of the Polynesian Labourers Act of 1868 and could not be sanctioned. As the island where Mr. McKinlay's fishing station was established was in Queensland waters, and formally annexed to this colony, he could not comprehend wherein lay the illegality of employing the kanakas there; but of course, he had to submit to this peculiar interpretation of the Act. This led to his engaging Fraser Island blacks for the work; eight male and two female aboriginals were engaged, in the presence of the shipping-master, the boys to receive £1 a month, together with clothes, rations, and tobacco.[73]

---

[71] QSA ITM17674, Letterbooks of despatches to the Secretary of State for the Colonies, 1875[3498] p. 471.
[72] QSA ITM858490.
[73] *Queenslander* 2 October 1875 p 6.

In a letter to the editor of the *Queenslander*, of 5 June 1875, John Campbell alerted the Queensland government to the loss of revenue by not controlling and regulating the pearl and bêche-de-mer fisheries through licensing of boats and other forms of revenue raising:

> There is another source of revenue in the North at present neglected, which ought to realise at least another half-million sterling of revenue. I mean the pearl and bêche-de-mer fishery. It is but lately that that fishery has excited foreign attention, but when pearl-shells reach the price of £260 per ton and bêche-de-mer some £140 per ton, some notion of its value may be formed. It appears there are many old vessels fit for no other trade being despatched from Southern Ports and anchored on our Northern shores, these serve merely as store-ships, and for their crews to live in, their numerous boats being despatched every tide to the neighbouring reefs to pick up the bêche-de-mer. Diving dresses are also introduced for pearling in deep water. Under all circumstances, it ought to be as great a source of production as our gold fields, and a revenue from the fishery much easier collected. ... let every vessel employed in the fishery pay a license of from £20 to £100 according to her tonnage; and cheap enough-too, considering how many dutiable goods she consumes in our waters without contributing one farthing to the revenue.[74]

Following on from the above, the *Brisbane Courier* provided a vignette of Somerset dated 10 July 1875:

> Messrs. Moodie, Munro, and Summers' fleet, consisting

---

[74] *Queenslander* 5 June 1875 p 9.

of a handsome centre-board cutter and several boats, arrived from Sydney and commenced operations on the shelling ground. They, with all others in possession of diving apparatus, have been doing well, working over the ground that was fished last season. The export since, including April of this year, to date, shows, pearlshell, 45 tons, bêche-de-mer, 15 tons. I can count fifteen different outfits at present shelling in the Straits, and four or five bêche-de-mering. This will represent a white population of about 50 men, and 400 or 500 islanders and Straits' natives. The South Sea men, after a little practice, become quite accustomed to the diving dress, and, with three or four exceptions, there are no white divers here now.[75]

On 7 May 1877, at Somerset, H. M. Chester reported on the Pearl Shell Fisheries in Torres Strait.

There are now sixteen firms engaged in the fishery, employing 109 vessels and boats, 700 natives and 50 Europeans. Sixty-three boats are fitted up with diving apparatus and the amount of capital is about £40,000. 1875—280 tons shell at £180 per ton, value £50,400. 1876----460 tons shell at £110 per ton, value £50,600.[76]

The first attempt to regulate the pearl-shell and bêche-de-mer industry in Queensland waters was in 1879 with the introduction of the Pearl-shell and Bêche-de-mer Fishery Bill by the Palmer government. Palmer said the bill was introduced by the government to do away, as far as they could, with the irregularity and lawlessness among the parties principally

---

[75] *Brisbane Courier* 27 July 1875 p 3.
[76] *Journal of the Legislative Council*, 1st Sess., 1879 Vol. 27 pp 903-904. Chester like Aplin makes no mention of the Bêche-de-mer industry of the time.

engaged in the pearl-shell and bêche-de-mer fishery trade about the Barrier Reef, and the islands that had come under the dominion of the colony. This bill provided for the employment and regulation of the engagement of Aboriginals.[77] When the bill reached the Legislative Council, the Postmaster-General said there would be considerable opposition to the measure;[78] and the Governor intended to ascertain during the recess the opinion of the Imperial Government concerning the power the Queensland Legislature had to pass such a Bill. The Colonial Office advised the governor that the Bill required a right of appeal clause and clauses 11, 12, 13 and 14 offended other colonial legislation.[79] Consequently, the bill was discharged from the paper, and rejected by the upper house.[80]

The following is from the report on the Torres Straits' Fisheries by the Resident Magistrate, at Thursday Island, 24 April 1879, which was laid before Parliament:

> The available adult population of these islands is employed by the occupants of the various stations as swimming divers, under the Masters and Servants Act; and the old men, women, and children, receive supplies of food in seasons of scarcity. The pay of these aboriginals is 10s per month, and their engagement is for one year only, out of which they are usually allowed a spell of two or three months during the rainy season but are paid for the full time. Payment is made either in my presence or that of the Shipping Master and consists

---

[77] Hansard LA 1 September 1879 p 1523 & 14 July 1879 p 766.
[78] This was in the form of a petition to the Qld parliament by Mr. Archer on behalf of certain residents of Sydney; *Journal of the Legislative Council*, 2nd Sess., 1879 Vol. 28 p 1315-1317. *Morning Bulletin* 22 July 1879 p 2.
[79] *Journal of the Legislative Council*, 1880 Vol. 30 Part II p 855-856.
[80] Hansard LC 24 September 1879 p 388. See correspondence on this at Qld Parl. 1880 V & P Vol. II p 1161.

of slop clothing, blankets, knives, hatchets, beads, &c., charged at reasonable prices-the owner, in most cases, giving a present in addition. If dissatisfied with what they receive, the natives seek a more liberal employer, thus the competition for their services is alone sufficient to secure them fair treatment.

They are well-fed, and by no means overworked. Fatal accidents from sharks occasionally happen, and the work of diving is not conducive to longevity; but the loss of life from those causes is more than counterbalanced by the decrease of infanticide and in the mortality amongst infants, due to the more regular supply of nourishing food.

The rest of the hands employed consist of South Sea Islanders and Malays, with a few Lascars and Chinese. The former sign articles in Sydney for a term of from one to three years, and receive wages varying from £12 per month, with a lay, for divers, to 30s per month for pump-hands and seamen. These men return to Sydney at the expiration of their articles, and after a few weeks on shore, ship again for the fisheries.

The Malays and Lascars sign ship's articles to work at the fisheries, before the Shipping Master at Singapore, who also takes care to secure for them fair wages, a proper dietary scale, and their due return to Singapore on expiration of the articles. The Chinese are employed as carpenters, cooks, and servants. They receive high wages and are fully able to take care of their own interests.

About two years ago an attempt was made to import what are known as 'green hands' direct from islands in the South Seas, by a license under the Pacific Islanders Protection Acts of 1872-5, granted by his Excellency the Governor of New South Wales, the inducement being economy in the matter of wages; but it proved more expensive in the end and has not since been renewed, for the loss of life owing to change of climate and food was so great that the men had to be sent home long before their time expired.

The boats employed in the fisheries are divided into two classes, viz., registered, and licensed. The former are required to have regular ship's papers and crews engaged on ship's articles under the Merchant Shipping Act of 1854.

The following is the statement of boats and men employed in the fisheries, Torres Straits:

Owners	Colony	Station Location	Whites	Natives
Jas. Merriman	NSW	Albany Island	5	114
Lamb and Parbury	"	Wai Weer Island	2	77
O'Hagan & McAlister	"	Banks Island	2	30
Joseph Tucker	"	Jervis Island	3	41
Craig Bros.	"	Endeavour Straits	2	60
F. W. Summers	"	Possession Is.	2	68
John Bell	"	Jervis Island	3	57
Moodie and Munro	"	Goode Island	3	34
J. Stevens	"	Albany Island	2	26
J. Cussen	"	Possession Is.	2	20
J. Walton	"	Barrier Reef*	1	46
P. Cadell	"	Jervis Island	1	33
P. Jardine	Qld	Somerset	3	68
B. Raff	Qld	Thursday Island		9
		Total	31	683

*   Bêche-de-mer fishing. The estimated capital invested is £35,000. The produce of the fisheries from 1st May 1877 to 30th April 1879 was 864 tons 6cwt 2qr pearl shell (live); 10 tons 17cwt 1qr 24lb dead; and 108 tons 2cwt 1qr bêche-de-mer.[81]

The annual report for the year 1879-80 of Mr. H. M. Chester, Police Magistrate, Thursday Island, showed an increase in bêche-de-mer fishing as follows: the number of men employed at the three stations (Barrier Reef, Murray Island, and Darnley Island), was 109 with a catch 50 tons 16 cwt. 1 quarter and 10 lbs. of product, valued at from £40 to £90 a ton.[82]

Boats and Men Employed in Bêche-de-mer Fishery.[83]

Owner	Colony	Fishing Station	Boats	Whites	Non-Whites	Aboriginal
W Walton	NSW	Barrier Reef	9	3	7	35
Bruce & Pitt	NSW	Murray Island	2	1	2	17
L Christensen	Qld	Murray Island	3		5	11
Tate & Williams	Qld	Darnley Island	3		2	12
B More	NSW	Murray Island	1		2	12
		Totals	18	4	18	87

THE PEARL-SHELL AND BÊCHE-DE-MER FISHERY ACT OF 1881.

In July of 1881, the Pearl-shell and Bêche-de-mer Fisheries Bill came before the House. The Colonial Secretary said the bill had been before the House in different shapes for two sessions past, commencing in 1879. The bill was very necessary, as there were a great many irregularities constantly arising in

---

[81] *Australian Town and Country Journal* 28 February 1880 p 23.
[82] *Morning Bulletin* 29 July 1880 p 2.
[83] Qld Parl. 1880 V & P Vol. II p 1158.

connection with the fishery, and consequently a great loss to the colony. The greater part of the capital employed on the fishing boats belonged to New South Wales. It was with the view of stopping those irregularities and of raising revenue that he introduced this bill and pressed it on the attention of hon. members. Concerning native labourers, that was the aboriginal natives of Queensland — a great many irregularities had taken place. He knew of several instances in which the offenders had not been got or punished, although there was substantial proof that both male and female natives had been taken up to these fisheries without leave or licences having been obtained. The fee for the licences would be less than under the former bills, the change being in deference to suggestions from Thursday Island. Native labourers and Polynesians were fully protected by the bill.[84]

This Act took effect from the first day of January 1882. The Act stipulated that it shall not be lawful to employ any ship or boat in the fishery within the colony, or within one league to seaward of any part thereof, unless such ship or boat was licensed and that the principal officer of Customs at any port may grant such license. Section 11 provided that it shall be unlawful for anyone to employ Polynesian or native labourers in the fishery except under a written agreement recorded in the Custom House or shipping office nearest to the place where it is intended to employ them, or under a license issued under the provisions of the Pacific Islanders Protection Act of 1875. All engagements of Polynesian or native labourers made out of Queensland were to be strictly in accordance with the shipping laws of the colony or country where made, and any master or other person who employs any Polynesian or

---

[84] *Telegraph* 27 July 1881 p 2.

native labourer in the fishery otherwise than as prescribed, or who fails to produce the agreement of any Polynesian or native labourer when required to do by an officer of Customs or member of the police force, will be liable to a penalty not exceeding £10. Clause 12 provided that, in the event of any Polynesian or native labourer who had been employed in the fishery being discharged or left by any master at any place without the written permission of the nearest police magistrate or principal officer of Customs, all expenses incurred by the Government in the maintenance of such labourer, or in providing him with a return passage to his native island or to the place from which he was originally brought, shall be chargeable to such master, and may be recovered in a summary manner; and that no license shall issue for any vessel in charge of such master until the same has been paid. Under section 13, all deaths and desertions of Polynesians or native labourers employed in the fishery were to be forthwith reported by the master or employer to the principal officer of Customs nearest to the place where they occur, under a penalty not exceeding £10 or less than £5. The requirement for a written agreement of employment between the employer and the Aboriginals, recorded at the nearest Custom House or shipping office, was seen as overcoming the practice of dragooning Aboriginals into the service of the industry.

The following letter from the sub-collector of Customs, Cooktown of 2 March 1882 may assist in understanding how the act was administered on the water:

> I report for the information of the hon. Colonial Treasurer an unseemly feature in the mode of recruiting natives to be employed under the Pearl-shell and Bêche-de-mer Fishery Act of 1881 which came under my observation on

the afternoon of 1 March 1882. About the end of January last two (2) cutters, tenders on the *Reindeer* and *Pride of the Logan* fishing smacks, left here for Townsville to obtain boys and returned, one on 28 February, the other on 1 March with 18 natives of both sexes varying in their ages from 9 to 40 years and procured I have reason to believe under very suspicious circumstances on Hinchinbrook and Dunk Islands and in the vicinity of the Johnstone River.

Having entered into a compact to recruit in company, upon arrival here they drafted these boys and gins after the manner of sheep each captain casting lots for nine (9) mixed sexes, without reference to the inclinations or feelings naturally induced by the filial or friendly instincts of the parties concerned. Some of whom I know manifested a strong aversion to their separation. Amongst those who fell to the lot of Captain Webb of the *Pride of the Logan* was a girl 11 or perhaps 12 years old, a mere child comparatively, who must have received shameful treatment on the voyage between Hinchinbrook and Cooktown as one Steve Barry who belonged to the *Reindeer* tender proceeded on board Webb's vessel took forcible possession of this child, claimed her as his own and dragged her by the arm through the main thoroughfare of this town, despite my remonstrances until he lodged or secreted her in a public house incidentally for very discreditable purposes. I immediately wrote to the local Inspector of police calling his attention to this shameful exhibition of brutality who to his credit had her promptly conveyed from her hiding den and by the aid of the police magistrate kept in his custody until means are available of returning the girl I fear in an outraged state to her native island.

On the following day, the remaining 17 were engaged before me by the masters of the *Pride of the Logan* and the *Reindeer* under the Pearl-shell and Bêche-de-mer Fishery Act of 1881. Such discreditable circumstances indicate a necessity for vigilant supervision in administering the act in northern Queensland until at all events some respect for its regulations is inculcated by meting out an exemplary measure of punishment to those whose illegal practices breach its enactment and who appear inclined to ignore every law civil and criminal in carrying out their ungodly acts. The natives along the coast are, however, far better off when and in most cases are willing to be usefully employed but I would point out that the mode of obtaining their services should in the interests of common humanity be more legitimately pursued than indiscriminately decoying them at every convenient spot along the coast and its islands irrespective of age or sex.

The licence fees received at this port to date under the Pearl-shell and Bêche-de-mer Fishery Act amount to £136 10s. and will in all probability before the year ends reach or exceed £200 and as this is the central and principal port of call for vessels exclusively engaged in the bêche-de-mer trade the license fees for two (2) years at least would cover the cost of a vessel 10-ton cutter without which I respectfully submit I am powerless to prevent or even check abuse of the provisions of the act referred to in the vicinity of this port. Fahey[85]

However, the following letter to the editor may be of interest:

---

[85] QSA ID ITM847064/DR77869 folio 156

A mere nominal tonnage tax should have been deemed sufficient where there is so much outlay, risk, and danger, for often very paltry returns. The reefs on the mainland coast have been so long and steadily worked that the fish now require time for natural increase and growth, and it is, therefore, necessary for us to push northward, and towards the coast of New Guinea and the adjacent islands. We are warned, however, by the naval officers who represent British justice, that we cannot expect protection there; while if any of us, when protecting our lives or property, happen to take the life of a native, we shall be seized and carried to Levuka or Sydney for trial. Even if we escape with our lives, we shall be ruined by loss of time and property, through the operation of this one-sided kind of law. Our transactions with the natives have been uniformly friendly and fair, but we have had to be constantly on our guard against their thieving propensities and their treachery and have been at times compelled to protect ourselves and recover our property by force of arms, but we protest against the legitimacy of the charges made by some missionaries to the effect that we have been the aggressors.

If the Premier sent a Royal Commission of inquiry to the North, he would find that we, while honestly prosecuting our hard-worked avocations, have done more for civilisation by employing and well-treating Papuans and aboriginals than has ever been done by the salaried missionaries. Why should the missionaries say that a man's avocation makes him more ungodly and barbarous when we find crowds of natives fishing on the coast of New Guinea, directed by native teachers and protected by the missionary banner? We only want fair play in prosecuting our industry and defy the missionaries or naval officers to prove that we have not both instinctively, and from the necessities of our vocation, been careful, commercially and morally, to treat the natives in a friendly and fair way. W. Campbell, J. F. Miller, K. Christopher, J. L. Swords, A. Carstairs, J. W. Bolles, S. Barry, J. Browne.[86]

A report from the Police Magistrate at Thursday Island on the pearlshell and bêche-de-mer fisheries in Torres Straits for 1883 was laid before Parliament:

It states that 206 fishing vessels were licensed during the year, employing in all about 1500 men; 33 licenses were granted to occupy fishing stations. The yield of pearlshell was 621 tons, 207 tons less than the previous year. The quantity of bêche-de-mer exported was 118 tons, an increase of 81 tons on the previous year. The decrease in the yield of pearl-shell was principally owing to the increased depth of water in which the divers are now working, and the bad weather; but the drinking habits of the men engaged in the trade have caused serious loss to their employers, 27 new boats were added to the fleet during the year. The total revenue collected at Thursday Island during the year 1883 was £10,412.[87]

AN ACT TO PREVENT THE IMPROPER EMPLOYMENT OF ABORIGINAL NATIVES OF AUSTRALIA AND NEW GUINEA ON SHIPS IN QUEENSLAND WATERS.

---

[86] *Brisbane Courier* 31 October 1882 p 6
[87] *Sydney Morning Herald* 25 January 1884 p 8.

The next attempt at regulating Aboriginal labour was the enactment of the Native Labourers' Protection Act of 1884 (short title), which began: It is expedient to make better provision for preventing the improper employment of Native Labourers on vessels trading in Queensland Waters. In committee the Premier said:

> there were a large number of ketches which traded along the coast. They were not engaged in the fisheries, but in carrying goods, and he had reason to believe that they were the very vessels that committed most of the abuses the Bill was intended to remedy. He believed that they sometimes came down to the islands between Townsville and Cooktown and took islanders away up north. According to his information, there had been a great many bad cases of kidnapping. He then cited the case of eighteen natives of both sexes, varying in ages from nine to forty years, including a 12-year-old female who was handed over to police. The remaining seventeen were engaged by the masters of the vessels, under the Pearl-shell and Bêche-de-mer Fishery Act of 1881. The majority of the (pearl) shellers have long since seen the folly of engaging these men, and it is only the small bêche-de-mer fishers who continue to employ them. The matter has assumed such serious proportion that I respectfully submit the engagement of aboriginals from the mainland should be absolutely prohibited.[88]

In support of the Premier, the Minister for Lands (Hon. C. B. Dutton) said:

---

[88] Hansard LA 30 July 1884 p 208, abridged. See also letter of 2 March 1882, pp. 52-54.

> The unqualified condemnation by the hon. leader of the Opposition to this measure, on the ground that it would interfere with the success of the bêche-de-mer fishery, will not be agreed with by many members in this House. The natives have been grossly ill-used along the coast. A measure of this kind is absolutely necessary to control the ruffians who exist among white men, where they are positively without check. I believe this measure will have the effect of deterring villains from committing such acts as they have been guilty of in the past.[89]

The evil or inappropriate recruiting practice that the Premier was trying to overcome was the way bêche-de-mer fishers obtained labour to collect and process the sea slug. Since the task required many hands to harvest the product and the only readily available source of labour was free-ranging mainland natives, the trepangers shanghaied the Aboriginals by coercive techniques such as trickery, intimidation, or violence. Furthermore, the captain of the vessel kept no record of the abducted crew, which in turn led to other abuses such as poor treatment of the crew with the extreme possibility that the kidnapped crew might be abandoned without their wages and entitlements or left for dead. Consequently, stringent rules were prescribed with a draconian punishment clause inserted in the draft legislation:

> Clause 7 provides that any vessel violating the provisions of the Bill by carrying "any native labourer, with respect to whom the provisions of the Act have not been observed," shall be forfeited, and the master and owner shall be jointly and severally liable to a penalty not exceeding £500. There is no other provision practicable.

---

[89] Hansard LA 29 July 1884 p 186.

On the other hand, employing Aboriginals, even if by fraud, was seen as a greater good than an idle bush black, as it meant Aboriginals were gainfully employed. Since a benefit arose from bad practice, the penalty should be ameliorated accordingly.

That was the line of reasoning that prevailed in the Legislative Council, which led to the following penalty clauses in the Native Labourers' Protection Act of 1884.

6. If any vessel trading in Queensland Waters carries any native labourer with respect to whom the provisions of this Act have not been observed, the master and owner shall be jointly and severally liable to a penalty not exceeding one hundred pounds.

7. If the master or owner of any such vessel, or any other person, discharges a native labourer who has been employed on board of any such vessel or pays his wages otherwise than as is herein provided, he shall be liable to a penalty not exceeding twenty pounds.

8. If any such vessel arrives in any port in Queensland having a less number of native labourers on board than are carried on the ship's articles, the master and owner shall each be liable to a penalty not exceeding five and twenty pounds for every native labourer so deficient in respect of whom such master or owner shall not prove to the satisfaction of the Court that he has been prevented by circumstances beyond his control from bringing such native labourer to such port.[90]

---

[90] Supplement to the Queensland Government Gazette, 20 November 1884, No. 93, p 1737, 48 Vict. No. 20. See Hansard LC 30 September 1884 pp 109-111.

Charters Towers, June 17, 1885. The Hon. A. Rutledge, Attorney-General, addressed his constituents in the School of Arts, referring to the Native Labourers' Protection Act, which was designed to protect the aborigines of the north-eastern seaboard and said:

> This was another measure by which the Government proved itself to be the friend of the people and downtrodden humanity. He made special reference to the shooting of the blacks. He was prepared to admit the possibly necessary use of the rifle in the early days of the pioneer squatters, but it was absolutely unnecessary to use the rifle on board bêche-de-mer vessels. The number of man-stealers on the northeast coast had now become as rare as the man-stealers in the islands.[91]

Christian Christensen was charged with a breach of the Native Labourers' Protection Act of 1884. Mr. Barnett appeared for the accused, and submitted that the information must be dismissed, as the charge should have been brought within six months date of the commission of the alleged offence, which took place on 29 March 1886, whilst the defendant was master of the schooner *Rover*. The case was eventually dismissed; the objection raised by Mr. Barnett was sustained.[92]

Thursday Island, 22 September 1887. Mossby and Walker, two bêche-de-mer fishermen, were fined £60 for a breach of the Native Labourers' Protection Act in not engaging islanders before proper authorities. The shipping master could have had six more cases against them, but he considered that the fine would be a sufficient caution for the future to prevent

---

[91] *Brisbane Courier* 18 June 1885 p 5.
[92] *Darling Downs Gazette* 26 March 1887 p 4.

the taking of Aboriginals without engaging them before the proper authorities.[93]

The report for 1885 of the Government Resident at Thursday Island made the following observations on the Bêche-de-mer industry:

> In reference to the bêche-de-mer fisheries, I regret to say that I am not as fully informed as I should wish to be. It is chiefly carried out in boats, which resort to Murray, Darnley, and York Islands. Since the loss of the *Mavis*, I have not had an opportunity of visiting the fishing grounds; I gather, however, from what I see and hear, that Europeans are going out of this industry, and that it is passing very much into the hands of South Sea Islanders, who will require pretty close watching. There is not much margin of profit in it unless very cheap labour can be obtained. This, however, is secured in the native inhabitants of the islands in the Straits, who are glad enough to work for small wages in order to earn what is called their "tucker". I estimate that there are 500 men and boys employed in this business, of whom probably a third, though possibly a half, come from the mainland of Australia. I have reason to believe that there has been a good deal of quiet kidnapping in this business. In one case especially, I ascertained that a lot of mere children had been purchased from their relatives on the Jardine and Batavia rivers. They were subsequently brought from Darnley to Thursday Island, in order to be entered on shipping articles, but it was so evidently a case which required my intervention that I caused them

---

[93] *Sydney Morning Herald* 28 September 1887 p 10 & *Brisbane Courier* 28 September 1887 p 6.

to be taken back to their people at the expense of their so-called employers. I believe that this action has had a beneficial effect in checking the employment of mere children in the Bêche-de-mer Fishery and that it has also been the means of establishing more friendly relations with the native inhabitants of the mainland. It is far better that these incorrigible savages should be taught to earn their livelihood in the islands than to lurk about on the Peninsula for the lives of white men, and I hope to encourage their employment; but the children, who are really useful for the purpose of collection, must be protected.[94]

THE 1886 ACT TO AMEND THE PEARL-SHELL AND BÊCHE-DE-MER FISHERY ACT OF 1881.

The Colonial Treasurer said in the Legislative Assembly of 20 July 1886:

> In 1881 the principal Act was framed, and in the working of that Act certain imperfections have discovered themselves which this Bill intends to remove, the first having reference to the licence fees which are charged upon vessels engaged in this industry. The Bill now before hon. members provides that fees shall be-
>
> For every ship of ten tons burden, or less, the sum of £3.
>
> For every ship exceeding ten tons burden, the sum of £3 for the first ten tons, and the sum of 10s. for every ton or part of a ton above ten tons but not exceeding in all

---

[94] *Brisbane Courier* 30 March 1886 p 3. Thursday Island, Report of the Government Resident for 1885, Brisbane 1886.

twenty tons.

For every boat, the sum of 10s.

It is also intended in the amending Bill that every port at which licenses are issued shall be defined upon the licensed boat by a certain letter, a letter being assigned to each port, so that the port from which the licence was issued may be more easily traced. After the Act of 1881 was passed that Act dealt solely with the engagements of Polynesian or aboriginal labourers, and white labourers were not subsequently subject to any regulation. The act has now been amended to include any seaman or other person. The Bill is a short one, but it has been framed to deal with the chief grievances which have been represented in connection with the pearl-shell and bêche-de-mer fisheries. It has been framed from actual observation, that is to say, from representations made by the pearl shellers and bêche-de-mer fishers as to their requirements, and I am sure it will afford them great relief from the grievances of which they have complained since the Act of 1881 was passed.[95]

Mr. Hugh Milman, the Acting Government Resident at Thursday Island, prepared an annual report for the year 1886, which was laid before Parliament in July 1887. From this report the following observations were made on the bêche-de-mer industry:

> The bêche-de-mer fishery, Mr. Milman says, is chiefly prosecuted on the reefs lying on the eastward side of

---

[95] Hansard, LA 20 July 1886 p 92 & 189, abridged. [Assented to 4 September 1886] Supplement to the Queensland Government Gazette, 10 September 1886, No. 43 p 951.

Torres Straits, and is followed by some dozen white men, several South Sea Islanders, and also by the natives themselves, who in some instances are supplied with a boat, receiving half the take. A large number of natives from all the islands, as well as "Binghis" (as aboriginals from the mainland are called), are employed by the white men and South Sea Islanders owning the boats. That much kidnapping has gone on of natives from the mainland is undoubted, but there is no question that the natives so employed improve much in their general appearance and physique, after being a few months away from their homes, where they are half-starved and in a most miserable state. Many, however, of the abuses which this employment of native labour had led to have disappeared now altogether since the passing of the late Acts concerning them, and from the fact that the employers never know now when they may be dropped on for inspection; and I am in hopes of being able to arrange, with the assistance of the shipping master, that the dates for the termination of the agreements entered into by the several employers shall coincide, so that the resident here or officer of Customs can in the *Albatross* superintend the return of the boys—a matter I consider of much greater importance than the method of engagement in the first instance, as I have not the least doubt that they (the mainland natives) have been, when their term of service has expired, turned adrift on the nearest and most convenient point of land, possibly among hostile tribes, who would at any rate rob them of their hard earned store of flour, &c, if they did not knock them on the head and eat them, after they had finished the poor wretches' flour.[96]

The Cooktown *Independent* provided the following observations on the Cooktown bêche-de-mer industry as it stood at the end of 1887:

> The bêche-de-mer industry, which once employed a considerable fleet and a huge number of white and coloured men, has now dwindled to a very small proportion, the exports for the 11 months being only 95½ tons (1,910 cwt.), value £7871. The industry was taxed when it should have been encouraged, and instead of protecting the enterprising fisherman; the Government treated them as the 'kidnappers and murderers,' described by lying Missionaries, who thus encouraged the natives to 'wipe them out' until only a few are left.[97]

REPORT OF THE GOVERNMENT RESIDENT AT THURSDAY ISLAND UPON THE WORKING OF THE NATIVE LABOURERS' PROTECTION ACT OF 1884.

The report of the Hon. John Douglas, the Government Resident at Thursday Island, on the working of the "Native Labourers' Protection Act of 1884," dated 27 August 1890, concluded as follows:

> 1. That no inspection and no supervision which it would be possible to apply, except at a largely increased outlay, would suffice to make the recruiting of Batavia River natives a justifiable expedient.

---

[96] *Queenslander* 30 July 1887 p 188.
[97] *Capricornian* 31 December 1887 p 8

2. That the indiscriminate punishment of natives is unjustifiable, but that the arrest and conviction of offenders, identified as such, is well-nigh impossible.

3. That the establishment of a mission and industrial station at the Batavia River would be the most effectual way of civilising these natives. There is a fine harbour there, with considerable forests of timber on the highest reaches of the river. The place swarms with natives, and it is an Alsatia for those criminals who have been described as fleeing from the defective justice of Torres Strait and its "Native Labourers' Protection Act". Naturally most treacherous and bloodthirsty, these natives of the Cape York Peninsula have been made still more revengeful and hateful by the injuries they have suffered at the hands of the white men.

It is said that discretion might be used in the recruiting of these natives and that those only who could be trusted to make good use of the permission to do so should be authorised. It is difficult to discriminate. The victims also of these outrages have been men who could not have been refused licenses. Williams was a good employer, so was Wilson, so was Sadleir, and so was Pim, yet they all suffered from these outrages, some with their lives, others with their property. I cannot see my way to the perpetuation of the practice of shipping these natives from the Batavia River unless some station is established there to supervise it. The same may be said of the Cape Grenville natives. There should be someone there on the spot to see to the agreements and how they are carried out.[98]

BÊCHE-DE-MER AND PEARL-SHELL FISHERIES OF NORTHERN QUEENSLAND — SAVILLE-KENT.

The following is an extract from the 1890 report of Mr. W. Saville-Kent, Commissioner of Fisheries on the bêche-de-mer industry:

> The fishery for bêche-de-mer is carried on chiefly by small luggers of five or six tons burden. These make daily voyages from the selected curing-station to the neighbouring reefs, which are exposed only at low water. The crews employed in gathering the bêche-de-mer consist chiefly of mainland aborigines, or "Binghis," as they are termed in the North, with a frequent admixture of Torres Straits and South Sea Islanders and Manilla men; these latter are frequently entrusted with the command of the separate boats. For the craft licensed from Port Kennedy, Thursday Island, the aboriginal crews are recruited to a large extent from the Batavia River, in the Gulf of Carpentaria; those employed on the boats fitted out from Cooktown are derived chiefly from the east coast districts. The licenses for boats taken out for the current year were in excess of last year's number. The returns in this direction show that 62 boats are now licensed from Port Kennedy, in Thursday Island, and 27 from Cooktown. To these are to be added some half-a-dozen which have taken out licenses at Townsville, Cairns, and Ingham. This gives a total of over 100 craft engaged in the fishery. A matter

---

[98] J. Douglas to Colonial Secretary, 27 August 1890, Qld Parl. 1890 V & P Vol. II p 1565.

demanding serious attention concerning the bêche-de-mer fisheries of Northern Queensland is associated with the employment of native labourers. Of late years, and in the Torres Strait district more particularly, outrages committed by these labourers, in which the boat-owners or their agents have been assaulted and lost their lives, or the boats with stores on board have been stolen, have become so frequent as to paralyse the industry to a very large extent. In the majority of cases, however, there is abundant evidence to show that the outrages have been committed with the simple object of obtaining loot, the many opportunities presented of gaining possession of a boat laden with stores proving an irresistible temptation to the uneducated native intellect.[99]

In a letter to the Chief Secretary on 30 October 1890, Mr. Douglas, the Government Resident at Thursday Island wrote as follows:

> I have lately apprehended several natives of the mainland of Australia who are more than suspected of being concerned in the murder of white men. All of these are intelligent young men, who understand English fairly well, and capable of acting as an interpreter; all these men might be indicted for crime on some show of evidence, but there is not the slightest chance of securing a conviction against any one of them. I propose, however, to utilise them us intermediaries to obtain the confidence of the tribes including the natives of the Batavia River. Through them, I hope to become acquainted with the leading men of the mainland. I should endeavour thus

---

[99] Qld Parl. 1890 V & P Vol. III p 727ff; *Brisbane Courier* 15 December 1890 p 7 & *Queenslander* 27 December 1890 p 1226.

to secure some recognition for a system of authority on the same principle as that applied to the natives on the islands of the straits — namely, by the appointment of native policemen, subject in the first instance to their superiors, and subject also to the police authorities here, from whom, through me, they would receive a small annual allowance. Mr. Acting Sub-Inspector C. Savage has suggested this mode of treatment. I should be authorised to draw on your department a sum not exceeding £60 a month for six months, the disbursements on this account to be certified in the usual way by vouchers. This expenditure would be under the following headings:

1. For the charter of a lugger when required, to be manned by natives under the supervision of the police. I should not always employ the same lugger, and would probably not make use of the same lugger for more than a month at any one time.

2. The pay, food, and clothing of six natives to be made use of as envoys and missionaries of goodwill among their acquaintances.

3. The subsidising of a few of the oldest and most important men among the tribes.

The leading idea behind my proposal would be as follows:

First of all, to gain the confidence of the natives, and then, when punishment of individuals became necessary, such punishment should be remitted to the native authorities, who would be held accountable for the administration of justice among themselves.[100]

On December 11, in reply to the above, Mr. W. E. Parry-Okeden, Under Colonial Secretary, wrote to Mr. Douglas as follows:

> The action taken by you as narrated in both (the above) letters is entirely approved. Your proposals as to establishing the beginning of a police system among the natives, the Chief Secretary does not think it practicable to authorise any punitive or coercive action without special legislation but is willing to sanction an expenditure of £10 a month.[101]

The following is the report of Acting Sub-Inspector C. Savage to the Government Resident at Thursday Island:

> Report on our efforts to civilise the natives of Cape York Peninsula. In the beginning, the difficulty was to obtain suitable natives to act as interpreters. Finally, they were provided by appointing two Jardine River natives who were acquainted with the English language as supernumerary trackers, with payment at the rate of 10s per month. Those men assisted in collecting the tribe at the Jardine River, in explaining what was required of the people, and in all the parleys which were held and through which in the end friendship was established. The chief was brought to Thursday Island, where he underwent a course of instruction, and when he had sufficiently understood what was required of him was taken back and made king, his subjects, and several visitors, natives of Prince of Wales Island being present.

---

[100] *Telegraph* 31 March 1891 p 2, abridged. *Telegraph* 17 April 1891 p 2.
[101] *Telegraph* 31 March 1891 p 2, abridged. *Telegraph* 17 April 1891 p 2.

The next place where the foregoing plan was repeated was at the Batavia River, at the mouth of which was found the chief of the Seven Rivers tribe. He was brought to Thursday Island for instruction. He proved to be a very intelligent man and was willing to learn. He was taken back and made king, in the same manner, as the chief of the Jardine River had been. Permanent camps have been established at the Jardine River and Seven Rivers, and large gunyahs have been built. Cocoanuts, sweet potatoes, pumpkins, and water melons have been planted, and are growing well at the Jardine River. The matter now stands thus. The natives at the Jardine and the Seven Rivers are aware that the Government takes an interest in them, is prepared to protect them, when necessary, from injustice, and expects their assistance in punishing crimes committed by their tribe. They have been shown how to make houses of bark and told that it is better for them to live in houses than to roam aimlessly about. They understand this completely, but whether they will continue as well as they are going on now remains to be seen. I believe, with constant supervision, they will.[102]

THE PEARL-SHELL AND BÊCHE-DE-MER FISHERY ACT AMENDMENT ACT OF 1891.

The amended provisions of the Act required that wages were to be paid in full in the presence of an inspector or officer of Customs or Shipping Master at intervals not exceeding three months and ships would not be allowed to carry more than

---

[102] *Telegraph* 31 March 1891 p 2. *Telegraph* 17 April 1891 p 2.

two gallons of spirits. Another most important, clause was the practical inspection of ship tackle and diving gear, to provide safety for those employed in what was now just as dangerous a calling as mining.[103]

The following letter from bêche-de-mer fishers sets out their views on the amendments of 1891 to the Pearl-shell and Bêche-de-mer Fisheries Act.

> To The Chief Secretary Brisbane,
>
> We, the undersigned fishermen connected with the Bêche-de-mer trade would respectfully bring under your notice the harassing conditions of Section 4 of the amended Act, whereby:
>
> 1. The wages of every seaman shall be paid in full, in coin, every three months in the presence of an inspector.
>
> 2. No master shall deduct any sum advanced, out of wages unless paid in the presence of an Inspector.
>
> 3. No master shall deduct any money for goods from wages.
>
> 1. We would point out that payment of wages every three months is quite unworkable when applied to floating stations (i.e., fishing carried on by large vessels, schooners &c.) which start on a cruise from 6 to 10 months at a stretch and extending from the reefs off Keppel Bay in the South to the reefs off Thursday Island in the North. The good weather for fishing is limited to a few months, and if the wages clause were strictly enforced and it became necessary for a vessel to knock

---

[103] Pearl-Shell and Bêche-de-mer Fishery Act Amendment Act, 1891.

off fishing in the middle of good weather and run in some cases hundreds of miles to port, the loss of time would be ruinous, and it means the complete shutting up of this industry. Further loss of time would occur when the seamen are paid, as they would certainly require a few days or weeks to spend their wages, and in the case of aboriginals if paid anywhere near their homes they would clear out in most cases for good. We are of opinion that the instructions issued to the inspector at Thursday Island by the Collector of Customs under date, Brisbane, 8 January 1892, are not applicable for floating stations, the work round Thursday Island being all done using fixed shore stations, whose locality is permanent. We, therefore, pray that for the carrying out of the portion Act, the inspector at Cairns be empowered to accept a bond for the due payment of the wages or accept from the agents of the vessels the wages due every three months; obviating the return of the vessel to Port and unnecessary loss of time. In such a risky trade it would be impossible for masters to carry an amount of specie equal to wages when insurances are at prohibitive rates.

2. With reference to the advances against wages, it will be very harassing to masters of vessels if they cannot be secured against advances made against wages, as it will often be found impracticable in the case of floating stations to obtain the necessary witness. We would pray that in the case of a floating station that the Inspector be allowed, as formerly, to sanction any reasonable advance, whether same be witnessed or not.

3. With reference to the clause stating that no money shall be deducted for goods, &c., &c. This will be

impracticable, applied to floating stations, as the men employed could never take out stores such as tobacco, matches, pipes, and clothing for an extended cruise. At present, it is the custom for masters to carry a supply of these articles. We would further point out that if this harassing condition is strictly enforced it will necessitate seamen being shipped at a lower rate of wages to cover these items. Of course, this does not apply to aboriginal labour, which is found in the abovementioned articles. We pray that the masters be secured against advancing necessary articles, provided the inspector satisfies himself that the seamen have actually had the articles, and a reasonable price be charged. We would further point out that the combining of the regulations for both the Pearling and Bêche-de-mer fishing trades in one Act is a great mistake, as the conditions are totally at variance. Pearling is worked from fixed shore stations within three miles of the Custom House, while Bêche-de-mer operations extend over 1000 miles of the coast of Queensland. In conclusion, we would respectfully request that the matter be attended to without any delay as the season when the vessels commence their cruise starts on or about the first of April next. W. Petersen, master, schooner *Curlew,* master, schooner *Griffin.* E. D. Beardmore, master of Forbes Is. station running four cutters and luggers. B. W. Bates, part owner, cutters *May,* and *Wave.*[104]

The Government received from the Hon. John Douglas, Government resident at Thursday Island, a copy of a report by Sub-Inspector C. Savage, on his visit to the eastern islands of

---

[104] *Cairns Post* 5 March 1892 p 2. See also *Cairns Post* 13 February 1892 p 2; 5 March 1892 p 3; 12 March 1892 p 3 & 20 April 1892 p 3.

Torres Straits, at the end of August 1892:

> At York Island, bitter complaints were made as to the treatment of mainland natives by bêche-de-mer fishers. It was alleged that the "boys" had to find food which they could and that some fishers had left "boys" on York Island, where they had to subsist on native fruits and what they could find on the reefs. A bêche-de-mer fisher at York Island had to keep a regular watch on his boats to prevent their seizure by "boys" left on the island by other employers of labour. Sub-Inspector Savage urges that searching inquiry be made into the matter.[105]

THE PEARL-SHELL AND BÊCHE-DE-MER FISHERY ACTS AMENDMENT ACT OF 1893.[106]

This act repealed the 4th clause of the Pearlshell and Bêche-de-mer Fishery Act of 1891 and provided for the wages of the men to be paid in full every six months rather than the previous every three months. The 1893 act also provided for the deduction from the wages of the men of one shilling for each month of wages paid to the finding of medical attendance and hospital accommodation for the men.[107]

Then the lugger *Wren* was found on the banks of the Skardon River, with the sails lying in the water, which was reported at Thursday Island, on 25 November 1893. Bruce, the owner of the *Wren*, had recruited eight natives from Bertie-Haugh, an inland cattle station on the Ducie River, occupied by Mr.

---

[105] *Telegraph* 17 October 1892 p 6.
[106] Supplement to the Queensland Government Gazette 30 August 1893. No. 124 p 1059. [Assented to 29 August 1893.] 57 Vict. No. 7.
[107] Hansard LA 18 July 1893 p 235.

Jardine. The crew of Ducie River blacks were alleged to have killed Charles Bruce and Captain Samuel Rowe. The incident provoked outrage in the Straits community against the mainland blacks. The government was powerless to render assistance, having no fast vessel at their disposal to institute inquiries. Bruce and Rowe had considerable experience with the natives, the latter being some time in charge of Jardine's fishing fleet, with quite a large number of natives under his command, with whom he always got along admirably. This incident made it six men killed by the natives in the waters of the Straits since July 1893, while another man was thrown overboard at sea but escaped. Feelings were running high at Thursday Island about the matter. Although murders were almost a monthly occurrence, the police had no boat at their disposal. The last patrol was sent out in an unseaworthy, leaky lugger which had to be bailed out with buckets day and night. There were insufficient police to carry out proper searches, and many believed that the government should keep the police in a smart lugger patrolling the coast in quest of these murderers. And further, it seemed a remarkable coincidence that murders had become quite common since the formation of a mission station amongst the natives at Batavia River.

On December 13, the police returned from the Ducie River where they were completely routed by the natives. Mr. Robert Bruce and senior constable Conroy narrowly escaped in their lugger, but without their ten native trackers. During the afternoon nine trackers, fully armed and another unarmed, were sent in search of the native camps, leaving Bruce and Conroy in the lugger. Shortly afterwards, a sharp engagement between the trackers and the blacks was apparent by the number of shots being fired. A large number of natives were seen on shore, many of them being armed, but there was no sign of the trackers. Bruce and Conroy, having only a revolver in their possession, pulled the lugger into midstream, when a large body of natives appeared on the opposite bank and commenced throwing spears at the lugger. Bruce and Conroy made the best of their way down the river under cover of darkness, the natives following for some distance, and still throwing spears occasionally. They then returned to Thursday Island. [108]

Then the *Brisbane Courier* of 15 December 1893 ran an article from the *Torres Strait Pilot:*

> Eight murders and several attempts thereat in about six months is a foul record unbeaten in Queensland history, and we fear very much that the pace will be kept going just as strong unless the manner of dealing with the mainland natives is completely changed. The first step towards this should be the abolition of the Mission Station at the Batavia, for we feel it is something more than a coincidence that the murders which had ceased for two years have commenced afresh as soon as the influence of the Mission Station is being felt. The next step should be the placing of the whole of the mainland under the control of Mr. Sub-Inspector Savage with full powers to deal with the native question; that officer of course to be relieved of office work and supplied with a vessel and a sufficient complement of men to carry out his work thoroughly. To support these views, we will review the history of native murders since the foundation of this paper in 1887, the previous records being unreliable:
>
> 1887: February—R. Goodshaw, a prospector, murdered

---

[108] *Brisbane Courier*, 28 November 1893, p.5 and 15 December 1893, p 5.

on the mainland.

1888: August—Charles Mogg, bêche-de-mer fisher, killed at sea.

1889: July—John Williams, bêche-de-mer fisher, killed at sea.

1890: April—W. Wilson, bêche-de-mer fisher, assaulted and left for dead.

1890: May—Charles Weir, murdered, at Haggerstone; desperate attempt made to murder Charles Burstow and Dan Maynard at the same place.

1890: September—Three natives of the *Rebecca* murdered.

1890: September—One of the crew of the *Teatfish* murdered at the Seven Rivers.

The above does not include the murder of Martin Oien in New Guinea or of Watson at the Coen, nor the larcenies of various boats, including three luggers. During those years there was a native police camp at Paterson whose duty it was to keep the natives in control. Despite this, the murders continued. The wholesale "dispersing" of the natives did no good, for it only made murderers of many innocent ones whose breasts were filled with desires for revenge for the hunting they have received or the death of their near and innocent relatives. The guilty natives invariably escaped, for a guilty conscience taught them to be on the alert and ever ready for a fly into the bush.

Paterson camp was disbanded at the end of 1890, and Mr. Sub-Inspector Savage took in hand the mainland natives. He paid periodical visits to their camps and enlisted the sympathy of the chief and tribe, whom he held responsible for the good behaviour of the natives of the tribe. The natives who engage from this port in the fishery are all known, as they have to be brought in here to be shipped when their descriptions are recorded. Thus, it was the police who knew the various murderers who were at large, and they, at once set about to have them dealt with, but using every caution not to quarrel with the tribe. The chief was interviewed and strengthened in his position as supreme in his edicts so long as they were in accord with common justice. A brass chest plate and a suit of clothes, with occasionally a few stores, had a wonderful effect on the various chiefs. Good seed having been sown, and the sympathy of the chief and tribe enlisted, it is understood that the police demanded the capture of the various natives who had been "wanted" for some time. These were captured, and then the chief was called upon to give them a proper trial and if satisfied of their guilt to punish them. It is not generally known, but it is said to be a fact, that the police thus had punished some of the ringleaders of the 1890 school of murderers. It was not legal probably, but it was perfectly legal from a native point of view, and certainly most sure and permanent in its good effect. Every native felt that if he committed a crime, he would be captured and summarily dealt with if he returned to his tribe, whereas if he did not return, he would be slaughtered by the neighbouring tribe. The results of this tribal law prove that it had a splendid effect on the natives, for not a single murder occurred from the time it was instituted until the present year. When the mission station was formed in 1892 the police gave up their work to the missionaries, and what has the result been?

Even more disastrous than it originally was. As the influence of the missionaries began to spread the natives became less inclined to work, becoming "educated" and lazy. Working for bêche-de-mer fishers became more irksome. It was not in the province of the missionaries to preach stern and speedy retribution if any murder was committed, or to instil into the chief the necessity to try and condemn any native who was guilty of a severe crime. Add to this the absence of the fear which had been created by the police, and it is easily understood that the native soon drifted back to his old state of having no respect for the white man, or no feeling regarding the rights of man to man. One or two murders were committed, and the police were sent to investigate. Their hands were tied by the very presence of the mission station. They dare not now ask the chief to see that the murderers were punished, for it was contrary to law, and the fear existed that the missionaries would put a noose around any man's neck who supported or urged what was contrary to law, but perfectly justifiable under the peculiar circumstances. The murderers were never made to pay the penalty for their misdeeds. They ran at large, disseminating evil. Quite as a natural sequence other murders followed until the number of them has become a foul blot on the authorities, who are incapable of checking others or of dealing with the known perpetrators.

The following terrible record for a few months shows the truth of this assertion:

1893: May—George Waters, bêche-de-mer fisher,

murdered at Forbes Island.

June—Kintu and Pascual, bêche-de-mer fishers, murdered on the mainland.

July—Hilario, Anastasio, and Julius, bêche-de-mer fishers, brutally assaulted. The latter died in the hospital.

October—H. Nicholls, bêche-de-mer fisher, thrown overboard at sea.

October—Peter Mobeck and Martin Oien, bêche-de-mer fisher and storekeeper, butchered at sea.

November—Charles Bruce and Samuel Rowe, bêche-de-mer fishers, disappeared mysteriously.

We abhor the very thought of having a native police camp on the Batavia, but this is certainly better than allowing such wholesale slaughtering to go on.[109]

The following article from the *Brisbane Courier* of 19 December 1893 under the headline, Bêche-de-mer, was said to be reportage from a Thursday Islander:

> The visitor stated that the bêche-de-mer industry could not be carried on under existing circumstances—that is by the employment of natives—without being attended with murder. Several reasons were assigned for this, one being that the natives got homesick and as they are not used to the water their work becomes oppressive. The chief source which leads up to the many murders, however, is the stealing of native women by the coloured men in the bêche-de-mer boats. Then, again, if the natives

---

[109] *Brisbane Courier* 15 December 1893 p 5. *Telegraph* 15 December 1893 p 4.

are employed to get firewood and water for the boats, and the boats attempt to get off without paying for the work done, the natives take their revenge.

While Sub-Inspector Savage, who is now clerk of petty sessions at Thursday Island, had the time to make periodical patrols along the east and west coast of Cape York Peninsula, he had the natives in complete subjection. When a wrong was done to the natives by outsiders, he endeavoured with the assistance of the chiefs of the tribe to sheet the charge home to the culprit, and in turn, if a wrong was done by the natives to outsiders he used to insist upon the chief of the tribe punishing the offender in a manner which suited the nature of the crime. This worked well, and few if any murders were then heard of. As the patrols of the police to the mainland have had to be discontinued, the onus of keeping the peace amongst the natives has fallen to the Batavia River missionaries. These people, whose intentions are good, know little or nothing of the cunning of the natives, especially when seeking to revenge a wrong, and consequently, they have little power to prevent outrages.[110]

In the letter given below to the Colonial Secretary, Douglas is said to have dealt with the subject of the above bêche-de-mer outrages:

Government Residency,
Thursday Island, Torres Straits,
16 December 1893.

They have occurred almost invariably in boats or on

---

[110] *Brisbane Courier* 19 December 1893 p 5, abridged & *Western Star and Roma Advertiser* 23 December 1893 p 4.

stations wholly manned or carried on by native labourers. The cases I refer to are generally those in which there is a starvation allowance for food. I have, however, known cases where murder has been committed by the natives in pure revenge for personal injuries and insults. But in the majority of cases, the moving cause in the perpetration of outrages is the desire to return home. But whether they are fed well or ill, whether they are treated badly or not, there comes over them, long before the expiry of their legal agreement, an irrepressible desire to return to their own country and their tribal usages. They talk of this among themselves. Then they agree to seize the first favourable opportunity, and they make a dash for freedom. If they get a chance, they run away with the boat, making straight for the mainland, landing anywhere they can, and abandoning the boat. If they find they cannot do this without killing their master, they avail themselves of the first opportunity and knock him on the head or pitch him overboard.

Then, as to the industry. It is conducted almost invariably by men who have only small capital, and not the means to go into the pearl shelling industry. It is not a nice business. Life on board one of these boats, or at the stations on the islands which are resorted to, is unspeakably squalid and dirty. For some men, however, it has an attraction, and there is often associated with it a good deal of illicit intercourse with native women. It is altogether a nasty, stinking business, and at the present time, it yields very small profits to anyone connected with it. It may be asserted; indeed, it has been broadly asserted by the local Press, which is of an exceptionally unprincipled and inexperienced type that the present outbreak of atrocities is due to the presence of the Moravian missionaries under the auspices of the Presbyterian Federal Church at the Batavia River. It is further stated that the hands of the police are tied by the fact that the missionaries have impeded their action and checked their efficiency. The statements thus made are most untrue, and most preposterous. The missionaries have done all they could to facilitate the arrest of offenders. The arrest of Harry Nicholls' would-be murderers was made by them and could not have been made without them. The police, moreover, are just as zealous as ever, though they have been nearly worked off their feet. The police have always acted most willingly and zealously, and, on their behalf, I most indignantly deny that they have on any occasion hesitated to do their duty when called upon to do so. Indeed, both Mr. Sub-Inspector Savage and Senior-constable Conroy have suffered seriously in health from the hardships, they have sometimes had to undergo while camping out. It is very evident to me that it will be necessary to adopt some means to stop these outrages. It can be best done, I believe, by checking the present system of recruiting; by making strict scrutiny into the character of those by whom they are recruited; and by not allowing the mainland natives to be worked except in combination with other nationalities. In the meantime, I propose not to allow natives from the mainland to be shipped except in boats where there is a sufficient proportion of South Sea Islanders, Malays, and Japanese to render their presence harmless. John Douglas.[111]

---

[111] *Brisbane Courier* 3 January 1894 p 6 & *Telegraph* 3 January 1894 p 5. See also Editorial, *Brisbane Courier* 4 January 1894 p 4; *Mackay Mercury* 1 January 1894 p 3 & *Mackay Mercury* 11 Jan 1894 p 2.

Gulf Murders — Evidence of Sub-Inspector Savage.

At an inquiry recently held by the Hon. John Douglas, Government Resident at Thursday Island, in connection with outrages by mainland blacks, Sub-Inspector C. Savage gave evidence to the following effect:

> I have been stationed in Torres Straits since 1885. A native police camp was established at Paterson soon after the erection of the telegraph line. After the native police left, I took a more intimate share in the control of the mainland natives. The area of my influence extended from Paterson to a little below the Skardon, including the natives of the Jardine and Seven Rivers districts. Was able to get on friendly terms with the blacks, though I had to adopt many a ruse. Finally, I managed to persuade two or three of the chiefs to visit Thursday Island, where everything was done to convince them of the power of the Government, and after kind treatment, they were taken back to their homes with presents in the shape of flour, tobacco, &c. Made frequent periodical visits to the mainland and kept up friendly relations with the tribes. At the Jardine, a garden was formed after a fashion — coconuts and a few sweet potatoes. There was a row at the Jardine, and that camp broke up and other camps were formed. My relations with the natives were such that I could always depend upon being able to arrest offenders or runaways, and the natives understood that they had to immediately report anything of importance.
>
> Local native policemen were appointed at the Skardon and the Jardine Rivers. At Red Island Point there was a camp, and from it, we could recruit assistant trackers

whenever required. On several occasions, runaway crews have landed there, and we have always received information through the Paterson telegraph station. In this way, several boats have been recovered. Did not extend my influence beyond the area mentioned, though I have made occasional visits to the Batavia. Senior-constable Conroy has recently been as far as the Pine River. Have never attempted any sustained influence beyond the north bank of the Batavia. A missionary station was established about two years ago near the mouth of the Batavia River. As regards my control of natives' affairs, the establishment of a missionary station has not affected me at all.

Have had less intercourse with the natives (Seven River tribes) since the establishment of the missionary station, but that is more owing to the increase of police work here. Do not regard the hands of the police as tied by the establishment of the mission station at Batavia River. The missionaries might try and put a noose around my neck or some of my men's necks, but they had never tried to do so to my knowledge. Have never heard of any complaint from the missionaries about the police. Senior-constable Conroy has not been so keen for mainland work as he used to be; don't know why. He has frequently asked me to send some other man. Conroy has done some excellent work on the mainland and passed through some hardships. Think his present condition of health is owing to the hardships he has passed through. The man has broken down.[112] It is not my opinion that the outrages of the last six months referred to in the article in the *Pilot*

---

[112] Senior-constable Conroy was stabbed to death by Frank Tinyana at Thursday Island on 2 July 1895, *Mackay Mercury* 17 September 1895 p 3.

of December 2 (1893) are due to the establishment of the missionaries. Waters's murder took place on the east coast at Forbes Island and had nothing to do, I believe, with the Batavia River natives. Kintu and Pascual were murdered at the Seven Rivers; one of the murderers was shot, and one is in custody. With regard to the assault on the Manilla men Anastasio, Julius, and another, I really cannot say whether it was committed by Gulf or east coast natives. I think they were Pine River natives. The lugger the men owned, the *Blackfish*, was notorious for women stealing. The attempted murder of Nicholls was, I think, perpetrated by Batavia River natives. There was one island boy in the crew, and two of the mainland natives showed a merciful disposition after Nicholls had been knocked overboard. The offenders, in this case were arrested by the police, and have been committed for trial. As to the murder of Peter Mobeck and Martin Oien. I am not surprised at the murder of Mobeck, but Oien was a thoroughly decent fellow. The murderers in this case are known and can be identified. They have not yet been arrested. They are 40 miles in from the Pine, to the south of Batavia. Re the supposed murder of Charles Bruce and Sam Rowe— this act was committed by Bertie-Haugh natives. They have not to my knowledge any communication with the mission station. Bêche-de-mer fishermen generally get their boys from one locality, and these boys work together in the boat. There are exceptions where the boys are mixed up. Mossby and Walker always mix their men.

Regard the mixing as the only safeguard for the employers. The more the mainlanders are mixed up with others the greater security there is for life and property.

Those boys who come from the mainland first appear at my office, where their names are entered in a register kept for that purpose. On many occasions, children and women brought up for shipment have been sent back to their country. A pretty strong check on illegal dealings by the bêche-de-mer men has been kept up. Very frequently natives who have been discharged at the shipping office are not returned to their country as they ought to be, and they are sent back by the police. Know the Batavia River. Have been there several times since the mission was formed. Think my last visit was in April 1892, when searching for Clarkstone's lugger. Have never given such information to the Press as would lead to the belief that these murders by natives are due to the influence of the missionaries. Do not think that the mission influence is directed in that line.[113]

Balanced against Sub-Inspector Savage's above evidence is the following report of Savage's activities regarding the control and policing of mainland Aboriginals in 1890:

> Mr. Sub-Inspector Savage, accompanied by Senior-Constable Conroy and a few native troopers, reports the *Torres Straits Pilot*, returned 14 December from their trip to the mainland. They took back Harry, the mamoose of the Jardine River. The Sub-Inspector was highly pleased to notice on his return that the natives had ably carried out his suggestions about forming a decent permanent camp. A native house has been erected for Harry; a larger building was also up for the accommodation of his subjects, while the ground in the locality was thoroughly cleared. Harry was, with considerable pomp, declared by

---

[113] *Telegraph* 7 February 1894 p 2.

the Sub-Inspector as the ruler of the district — a position which he has always occupied — and Harry returned his thanks and promised future good behaviour for his tribe. He was presented with a camp-oven, frying-pan, knives and forks, and other cooking utensils; but the most valuable prize was a brass plate with "King Yarra-ham quee" engraved thereon, which hung round his neck by a silver chain. Having disposed of this tribe, Mr. Savage started along the coast for the Batavia River. At the Seven Rivers, they spoke to a large camp of natives, and with the aid of Kio, the police tracker, they soon established friendly relations. Mr. Savage explained the object of the visit, hoping to pay them periodical visits of inspection. The mamoose, Charlie by name, has come back with Mr. Savage but will be returned laden with good things and high opinions, before the coming Christmas. He cannot speak a word of English, nor had he been near a white man's abode until brought into our midst. One of his first impressions on rambling about the Barracks was conveyed in the question he asked Kio, the interpreter: "Why white man could make the fowls stay about the house when in his country they all flew away and could not be caught?" Kio explained as best he could to the mamoose that the white man possessed a magical power which was sufficient to tame anything. Charlie will probably realise this after he has spent two weeks here as the guest of the Government. The rough edges of his savagery will be toned down a bit.[114]

A further interesting point of view was raised in a letter to the editor of the *Brisbane Courier* on 8 February 1894 regarding

---

[114] *Morning Bulletin* 16 December 1890 p 6. The reader is asked to re-read pp 70-71.

hon. Douglas' analysis of why the binghis resumed killing their bêche-de-mer masters:

> The letter from the Hon. John Douglas gives an insight into the real causes of these murders. Mr. Douglas is a little more verbose, and describes it as "an irrepressible desire to return to their own country and to their tribal usages." On that point, all are agreed. The preventive for this irrepressible desire is wherein I claim to differ from the hon. gentleman.
>
> A serious misstatement made by Mr. Douglas is chosen by you in your leader of 4th January to uphold that gentleman and his hobby—the mission. That is where Mr. Douglas states that "the police are, moreover, just as zealous as ever." At the informal inquiry held by the Hon. John Douglas, in which the hon. gentleman alone took part in the examination of witnesses, Senior-constable Conroy stated, "When the missionaries came, we did not care to go to the Batavia." At the same inquiry Mr. Sub-Inspector Savage stated, "Senior-constable Conroy has not been so keen for mainland work as he used to be, he has frequently asked me to send some other man." These voluntary admissions from two police officers completely refute Mr. Douglas's assertion that the police are "as zealous as ever". The officer invariably sent to the mainland actually begged his superior officer to send some other man. Mr. Douglas has not made this mistake willingly; it is his unfortunate inability to see and know things as they are which brings it about. The senior-constable referred to, and the sub-inspector, have made no secret to their friends for months past of their reluctance to carry on mainland work when the

mission was close by. The secret of this dread lay in the fact that the work they started before the mission came, and which brought about two years of absolute peace, was illegal, for it was an open secret they had known murderers punished by the natives themselves after a formal trial before the chief and the tribe. According to the police accounts, these trials were carried out with all the ceremony and pomp possible, to make them more impressive. With the mission at hand, illegal work by men paid to see the laws respected could not be thought of. The knowledge of certain punishment when they returned to their native tribe being abolished, the natives soon commenced their murderous doings.

This certainty of punishment will alone curb their "irrepressible desires." We presume this same "desire" existed during Mr. Savage's two years of peaceful rule or has it suddenly been created by the mission influence? With perhaps one or two exceptions these murderous natives were engaged by the same bêche-de-mer men in the same semi-starvation work—upon which it is noted they always fattened—with the same boats in the same localities and yet their "irrepressible desire" was restrained because they knew death was certain at an early date after their return to their tribe, and they had nowhere else, even if they had the desire, to flee to.

On the one hand, close the bêche-de-mer industry by cutting off the only labour possible, and your revenue decreases; ruin the great number of men now making their living by that industry, and you increase the number of unemployed, white and natives. The other picture—change the Batavia River mission into a police camp through which native labour can alone be recruited, and you will foster the bêche-de-mer industry, and also assist materially the shelling industry, and provide the natives with the means of earning a good living, while, better than all else, you will bring about a return of the peaceful era. This is unquestionably the view taken by almost every resident in this district, even amongst many who are just as humane and philanthropic as the Hon. John Douglas. A Justice of the Peace. Thursday Island, 21 January.[115]

It is not possible to reproduce here the full extent of the press coverage the editorial of the *Torres Strait Pilot*, published by the *Brisbane Courier* of 15 December 1893, generated over the blacks' killing whites who worked in the bêche-de-mer industry. The following in tabulated form is a summary of the newspaper coverage:

Newspaper	Editorial	Date	Theme
Mackay Mercury	yes	17/5/1890 p 2	Bêche-de-mer licenses to men of good character, strict Govt supervision
Mackay Mercury	yes	11/9/1890 p 2	Bêche-de-mer outrages, industry to blame
Mackay Mercury	yes	16/10/1890 p 2	The whites engaged in it, and their black servants are really at war
Brisbane Courier	no	15/12/1893 p 5	Reproduced *Torres Strait Pilot* Editorial
Brisbane Courier	Ltr to Ed	16/12/1893 p 5	Comments on *Pilot* Ed. Abolish bêche industry
Brisbane Courier	Article	19/12/1893 p 5	Binghis murders: homesick, work oppressive, stealing gins, failure to pay for work done
Brisbane Courier	Ltr to Ed	19/12/1893 p 5	T. Coventry, myalls not all bad, will work
Telegraph	yes	15/12/1893 p 4	Bêche-de-mer outrages, industry to blame & no supervision

---

[115] *Brisbane Courier* 8 February 1894 p 7.

The Bêche-de-mer Industry in Queensland

Queenslander	yes	23/12/1893 p 1209	Gin stealers should be punished by government & the Bêche industry investigated
Queenslander	no	23/12/1893 p 1235-6	Reproduced most of the above articles
Brisbane Courier	yes	4/1/1894 p 4	Called for an investigation into the Bêche-de-mer industry
Mackay Mercury	yes	11/1/1894 p 2	Wants the killing stopped & an investigation held
Mackay Mercury	no	11/1/1894 p 3	Reproduced *Torres Strait Pilot* Editorial
Brisbane Courier	Ltr to Ed	8/2/1894 p 7	A Justice of the Peace (see letter above)
Brisbane Courier	Ltr to Ed	9/2/1894 p 7	Vox Populi
Queenslander	Ltr to Ed	17/2/1894 p 329	A Justice of the Peace & Vox Populi
Telegraph	yes	17/2/1894 p 4	Called for an investigation into the Bêche-de-mer industry
Brisbane Courier	yes	9/2/1894 p 4	Rule of law must be established in the Bêche-de-mer industry
Brisbane Courier	no	21/2/1894 p 5	*Torres Strait Pilot* Re Douglas on profitability of bêche-de-mer
Brisbane Courier	yes	10/3/1894 p 4	On profitability of bêche-de-mer
Brisbane Courier	Ltr to Ed	10/3/1894 p 6	An Observer, on profitability of bêche-de-mer
Brisbane Courier	Ltr to Ed	10/3/1894 p 6	A Justice of the Peace, further comment on Douglas
Brisbane Courier	Ltr to Ed	6/4/1894 p 7	Fair Play, Reply to An Observer, Aboriginal crew not starved
Brisbane Courier	no	10/3/1894 p 4	Sending a reporter to investigate the bêche-de-mer industry
Brisbane Courier	no	10/7/1894 p 2	Report on working a bêche-de-mer vessel.

POLICE PATROL IN THE GULF

To exercise greater supervision over the bêche-de-mer fisheries it was decided to make an important change in the system of police patrol in the far North. The district of Thursday Island was extended to the adjacent islands and the eastern and western coasts of the Northern peninsula. The patrol would be accomplished by a steamer, the whole district being placed under the charge of Sub-Inspector Urquhart. The sub-inspector holds a master mariner's certificate. Sub-Inspector Cooper of the Coen succeeded Sub-Inspector Urquhart at Cloncurry. The destination of Sub-Inspector Savage, who was in charge at Thursday Island, has not been decided upon.[116]

REPORT OF THE GOVERNMENT RESIDENT AT THURSDAY ISLAND FOR 1892-3.

Hon. Douglas, Resident observed:

> For three years 1890, 1891, and 1892 not a serious offence had been committed. We became well acquainted with the natives, and a small distribution of flour and tobacco, which was authorised helped to cement a friendly understanding. It has been said by the current commentators of the local Press that these amicable relations were brought about by the police through the application of what has been called tribal law and that this influence has been broken down by a counter influence coming from the missionaries at the Batavia River. This supposed application of tribal law is, in my opinion, a pure figment of the imagination. It does not exist and never has existed. Such, however, is the effect, of the imagination, that it has been spoken about and written about as a sober certainty. Tribal law is said to be something of this kind: If a native committed an offence, ran away with a boat, or killed his employer, he was denounced to his tribe, and then condign punishment

---

[116] *Brisbane Courier* 5 May 1894 p 4.

followed; he was knocked on the head, or a spear was put through him. The police were supposed to try him first. It was not necessary to arrest him or to identify him. Inquisition was made, and then if the police were satisfied, he was, as it were, handed over to the secular arm. Tribal law was enforced, and the offender sooner or later disappeared—that was the idea; it was supposed to work well, to save a good deal of trouble, and to mete out a kind of rough justice.

There has been no doubt some cases of tribal offenders. Two of these I can speak of from personal knowledge—natives who stole firearms and terrorised their own people. These men were no doubt outlawed, and justly outlawed, by the police, and they were eventually dealt with rather summarily. One of them was killed by his countrymen, and the other was very pluckily captured by one of our trackers. He served a sentence in gaol, behaved in a most exemplary manner while serving his sentence, and escaped only a few days before his sentence would have expired. That man is still at large and is an outlaw. But as to this tribal law being enforced-it is a pure myth, an effort of the imagination and nothing more. It never has been enforced. The mainland natives have no notion of trying a man on any principles of evidence, though, of course, it might be quite possible to induce them to kill certain designated offenders. This tribal law business accordingly is, in my opinion, all moonshine, and need not be seriously discussed by anyone who does not wish to be considered a gobemouche. It follows that the supposed primary administration of tribal law so successfully applied, and its subsequent relaxation, through missionary influences, had nothing to do with the outrages which have lately occurred. These must be traced to specific and not to general causes. There was an outbreak of crime--an outrage was committed and the infection spread; another murder was committed, and that excited another. Altogether seven lives were, lost, three being coloured men, and four being Europeans.

The first of this series of outrages was that of Pascal and Kintu, two Manilla men, who owned the cutter, *Leonora*. They were murdered on the west coast of the Cape York Peninsula by two Batavia River boys whom they had shipped. The natives stole a gun. One of the offenders, being in possession of this gun, resisted capture by firing on the police and was himself shot. The other was subsequently arrested and was committed for trial, but the evidence depending on the imperfect statements of his tribesmen, no true bill was filed against him. He stated that the murder was committed because the Manilla Men took their gins away from them. The first information of this murder was received by the police on 5 June 1893.

The next outrage took place off Boydong Cay, on the east coast. Four Manilla men shipped seven Pine River natives in the Black Fish. The Manilla men, while sitting at supper, were attacked, but made a successful resistance, and the natives jumped overboard, swimming to shore. Conception, one of the Manilla men, was seriously wounded in the head by a tomahawk and died in the hospital. Of the natives, nothing has been heard since, and it is not known whether they are dead or alive. This outrage was reported on 24 July.

The attempted murder of Harry Nicol by throwing

him overboard was reported on the 4th of October. The offenders ran away with the boat to the Batavia River, where they were captured and are now awaiting their trial. The murder of Mobeck and Oien was reported on 24 October. From the scanty native information which has been gleaned in this case, it would appear that Mobeck knocked over one of the natives with the iron tiller of his lugger. The tiller was taken from Mobeck and used against him. He was then thrown overboard, and poor Oien, who was a perfectly innocent passenger, was treated in the same way. The perpetrators of this outrage are known and could be identified. They belong to the Pine River tribe, forty miles south of the Batavia River, and they could probably be arrested, but no evidence, could be obtained which would justify the expectation of a conviction, Senior Constable Conroy with a party of trackers was sent in pursuit of these offenders. He followed them for several days from camp to camp, but provisions falling short he had to make his way back to the coast without having effected a capture. The last outrage was that of Bruce and Rowe, reported on the 25th of November. Bruce had recruited eight natives from Bertie-Haugh; an inland station on the Ducie occupied by Mr. Jardine. He had been warned by Mr. Jardine that they were dangerous, and was advised not to have anything to do with them.

So much has been said and written on the subject that I do not propose to say very much more. I have already addressed to you a letter which sufficiently summarises my opinion as to its leading features. I attach a copy of it to an Appendix. The figures furnished by Mr. Hennessey, and published herewith, show that the industry at this port is in a languishing condition. It is impossible to supervise it properly. To do so effectually would cost more than it is worth. The shipping of natives may be controlled and if proper care is taken to mix them with other nationalities there will be less risk to life and property. I do not think that any good has come or can come from the Native Labourers Act in this district. Many white men have lost their lives at the hands of the natives. The natives have gained little or nothing from their schooling; their women have been debauched and appropriated; their young men have in too many instances been taught the accomplishments of drinking and swearing, and some tribes have been so decimated that there is nothing of them left but the old people and the young children.[117]

ABORIGINALS IN QUEENSLAND — MR. A. MESTON'S REPORT.

The Government of the day decided that it was necessary to inquire into the conditions of the Aboriginals to see if they were getting value for the money they spent. Mr. Archibald Meston, a friend of the aborigines who knew something of their ways, was given an amicus brief to report upon the matter. The report was to examine and inquire into the present condition of the mission stations and the native police stations; also, the bêche-de-mer and pearl-shelling traffic, and it was expected to contain information upon which the Government could act, not only by voting more money but by introducing

---

[117] Report of Government Resident at Thursday Island for 1892-3, dated 1894. Qld Parl. 1894 V & P Vol II p 907ff.

legislation dealing with the abuses which would come under their notice. The report on the Aboriginals of Queensland, by Mr. Meston (special commissioner under instructions from the Queensland Government), was presented to Parliament by the Home Secretary in 1896. Meston made the following observations on the bêche-de-mer industry:

> The coast blacks who have been out after pearl-shell or bêche-de-mer have not been subjected to a process of improvement, nor have they acquired a high opinion of the whites. Some of the bêche-de-mer fishermen treated them fairly, but there were others men who enticed blacks on board, worked them like slaves, treated them like dogs, and finished by leaving them marooned on a reef, or shot them, or landed them far from their own home on some strange part of the coast, where they would be certain to be killed by the first tribe they met. The kidnapping of women and nameless outrages were prevalent along the coast, and are not yet at an end. At several points, the blacks made bitter complaints of their men and women being taken away and never returned, and tales of shameful deeds were told to me by blacks who had been out fishing on the reefs, where they had no chance to get away. Occasionally bêche-de-mer fishermen were killed by aboriginals driven to desperation, and most of these so-called "murders by the blacks" were merely acts of justly deserved retribution. The trade has been conducted by too many in a reckless, immoral spirit, free from any sense of responsibility, and neither amenable to nor fearing any kind of supervision whatever. Hence the serious necessity for either placing the bêche-de-mer aboriginal labour under the most stringent regulations or refusing to allow

such labour at all under any conditions. A somewhat similar indictment is aimed at a section of the pearl-shell fishery, and the result is an exactly similar verdict. A recognition of the utter unfitness of civilised men to be allowed unfettered and irresponsible control over a savage race was the cause of inducing the Queensland Government to place the kanaka traffic and labour under such careful and stringent supervision as to reduce even the possibility of abuse of any kind to a minimum. A similar recognition of the abuse of aboriginal labour in the bêche-de-mer and pearl fisheries will doubtless lead the Government in an equally humane spirit of justice to an equally desirable result. At present the pearl-shell boats are nearly all controlled and manned by coloured men; a heterogeneous mixture of Javanese, Malays, and Polynesians. I saw at least 100 luggers with not a white man on one of them. Those men, as a class, are not fitted by either natural or acquired qualifications to come into contact with the mainland aboriginals—men, women, or children. One of the first effects on a black race of contact with a white one is to excite cupidity, involving degeneracy towards social and moral depravity that even sacrifices the virtue of the women in order that the cupidity may be gratified. It is a common practice for bêche-de-mer and pearl-shell boats to run down to some point on the coast where blacks are camped, send their boats ashore, and purchase a number of women, paying for them usually with flour and tobacco. These women are sent ashore before the boats depart. In some cases, the women were taken by force, and in the disturbance that followed one or more of the men were shot. Before the boats were prohibited from taking native women on board for a cruise, the abuses were of a much more serious character. The pearl-shell boats are a mischievous nuisance to the Batavia River missionaries. Even on the morning of my arrival at Mapoon, by way of the Ducie River, when crossing Port Musgrave, I saw a lugger just leaving the anchorage of the open beach about a mile behind the Mission Station. She had anchored there on the previous night, sent the boats ashore, bought half-a-dozen women, took them on board all night, and returned them next morning. Most of the blacks were away using the flour and tobacco which formed one of the terms of the contract. These practices are well known to the boys and girls on the Mission Station; and if the schoolgirls were not under proper control and guarded at night, the old men of the tribe would periodically dispose of them in a similar manner.

Recommendations:

1. The total abolition of the native police, and all police duty among aboriginals to be done by white men, with an unarmed tracker in localities where trackers may be necessary.

2. Absolute prohibition of all aboriginal labour on pearl-shell, bêche-de-mer, and tortoise-shell fishing boats under any conditions whatever.[118]

---

[118] Qld Parl. 1896 V & P Vol. IV p 723ff, abridged.

REPORT OF THE COMMISSIONER OF POLICE ON NORTH QUEENSLAND ABORIGINES AND NATIVE POLICE.

Mr. W. E. Parry-Okeden, Commissioner of Police, submitted his report on the Aborigines of North Queensland and on the native police stationed in that part of the colony, on 19 February 1897. The following are extracts:

> Mainland aborigines are not employed to any extent in the pearl-shell industry, as they are not reliable enough to act as tenders to divers or as pump hands, and are useless as dress-divers; but two or three owners of small boats employ a small number of them as what are called "swimming divers" in shallow water. These are mostly well-treated and are regularly shipped on proper articles and duly paid off at the Thursday Island shipping office.
>
> In the bêche-de-mer and turtle fishing, however, a considerable number are always engaged, and it is in this branch of the fishing industry that all the abuses and outrages so much heard of occur. The bêche-de-mer business is a dirty one but profitable, and seems to possess attractions for the lowest class of whites and Manilla men, who have no scruples whatever in dealing with their black employees.
>
> By a local arrangement among the Government officials at Thursday Island no mainland blacks can be shipped on the fishing boats until passed for the purpose by the officer in charge of police, but this and all other regulations are easily evaded by the following or similar methods. A bêche-de-mer man owning a mall vessel will sail from Thursday Island with two congenial ruffians (usually coloured men of nondescript nationality) shipped as mate and cook for Cape Melville or the Batavia, Pine, or Coen rivers. He will then by presents and promises induce as many blacks, male and female,

as he can carry to come on board, and with them, he will make for any island as near settlement as he thinks safe. There he will land all the blacks except four or five males, with whom he will proceed to Thursday Island, get them regularly shipped, and then make all haste back to his depot, where he will pick up the temporarily marooned blacks and sail for his ultimate destination—some islet or lonely sandbank in the Eastern Fields, in the Great North-east Channel, or far out on the Barrier Reef. Here he will erect his "smoke house" and commence real operations. Taking all the male blacks, he will sail to another sandbank perhaps fifteen or twenty miles distant, will there land them, and leaving them a small dinghy in which to reach the neighbouring reef, where the bêche-de-mer is to be collected, he and his mates will return to their headquarters, where they will revel in the society of the grass widows of the fish collectors, whom they will occasionally visit to bring in the fish obtained by them to the "smoke house." Meanwhile, the blacks will work patiently for a time, fed on a small allowance of "sharps" (an inferior kind of flour), and such fish as they can catch. Those that get sick die unrelieved and unrecorded, and they all live the hardest possible life, generally on the verge of starvation and frequently in want of water.

They weary of this after a time, and cast about for means of returning to their country, when perhaps the bêche-de-mer man and his mates will be suddenly tomahawked and thrown overboard, and the whole mob of blacks will return triumphantly to their country, where, having stripped and gutted the vessel, they will leave her on the beach to be presently found and towed into port by the *Albatross*. Or they will essay the voyage in the little dinghy when they will in all probability be drowned and never heard of, and they will even attempt escape by swimming. A case occurred in 1880, in which two boys and a gin swam from a bêche-de-mer station sixteen miles from reef to reef till they reached one near the Piper Lightship, where they were seen and picked up and landed on the mainland by the lightship's boat. But if no tragedy occurs and the blacks do not abscond, when the bêche-de-mer man has a sufficient cargo of fish he sails for the nearest point of the coast and there lands his blacks quite regardless of where they originally came from, giving them perhaps some tobacco and a few coloured handkerchiefs as the reward of months of work, and goes on to Thursday Island with the four or five regularly shipped blacks, who he virtuously pays off at the shipping office, and having realised his cargo will spend the proceeds in drink and debauchery.

It is hard to blame the blacks in this matter whatever they may do. Many of these bêche-de-mer men are the lowest of the low; they wield absolute power at the lonely fishing stations, and the moral and material welfare of their employees is for the time being entirely in their hands, and there is no doubt that they cruelly wrong and oppress the blacks who work for them and thereby provoke the so-called "atrocities."

There are two ways of dealing with the matter first, by absolutely prohibiting the employment of aborigines in the industry; this is the simplest and most inexpensive, and I believe the best, but it would mean the extinction of the industry, and probably, as a proposal, would meet with very great opposition. The second is to place a small steamer similar to the *Vigilant* in the Straits in charge of a police officer, who should be also an inspector of fisheries and a deputy-shipping master.[119]

---

[119] Qld Parl. 1897 V & P Vol. II p 23ff, abridged.

MEASURES RECENTLY ADOPTED FOR THE AMELIORATION OF THE ABORIGINES.

The Home Secretary, H. Tozer issued the following memorandum on 25 November 1897:

> In consequence of frequent depredations and many outrages committed by the aboriginals in Cape York Peninsula, which called in question the efficiency of the native police, the Commissioner of Police (Mr. W. E. Parry-Okeden) was directed to proceed north and personally inquire into the operations of that force, and to report generally on the condition of the North Queensland blacks. Mr. Meston's report was published just before the Commissioner of Police set out, and that of Mr. Parry-Okeden early in the present year. The result of these two reports was, first, the better working of the native police as a force equally and impartially protective of blacks and whites; and, secondly, the using of the overland telegraph stations as friendly refuges and food distribution centres for the tribes along the Peninsula. Both these changes have been already attended by gratifying results. The Aborigines Bill introduced in this session, deals with the question of the improvement of the aboriginals, and aboriginal half-casts, and their future protection, in an effective and comprehensive manner. It not only aims at effectually preventing a continuation of the errors of the past but contemplates preserving the aboriginal race from extinction.[120]

---

[120] Qld Parl. 1897 V & P Vol. II p 43ff, abridged.

AN ACT TO MAKE PROVISION FOR THE BETTER PROTECTION AND CARE OF THE ABORIGINAL AND HALF-CASTE INHABITANTS OF THE COLONY, AND TO MAKE MORE EFFECTUAL PROVISION FOR RESTRICTING THE SALE AND DISTRIBUTION OF OPIUM.[121]

The act was assented to on 15 December 1897 and the preamble read as follows:

> Whereas it is desirable to make provision for the better protection and care of the aboriginal and half-caste inhabitants of the Colony: And whereas great and widespread injury is being caused to the aboriginal and half-caste and certain other inhabitants of the Colony by the consumption of opium: And whereas the restrictions heretofore imposed by law upon the sale and distribution of opium are found to be insufficient, and it is expedient to make more effectual provision for restricting such sale and distribution, and for preventing the evils arising therefrom: Be it therefore enacted by the Queen's Most Excellent Majesty, by and with the advice and consent of the Legislative Council and Legislative Assembly of Queensland in Parliament assembled, and by the authority of the same as follows.

This act was intended to secure the wellbeing of the fast-disappearing aboriginals of Queensland. It combined a general and a specific object; the first, to make provision for the better protection and care of the aboriginal and half-caste inhabitants of the colony; and the second, to make more effectual provision for restricting the sale and distribution of opium. The opium

---

[121] Supplement to the Queensland Government Gazette, 16 December 1897, No. 149 p 1387. 61° Vict. No. 17.

provision was emphatic testimony to the injury wrought among the blacks by the opium habit, and it was remarkable that in the opposition since made to the Act, these anti-opium provisions found no ostensible objection. The provisions relating to the sale of opium were of a very far-reaching and drastic nature, and their enforcement entailed a certain amount of hardship; however, unless the greatest possible obstacles were placed in the way of procuring opium, it would be impossible to prevent the drug reaching the hands of the blacks, so long as those blacks who were addicted to the use of opium could obtain it, but little could be done to ameliorate their condition.[122] Be that as it may, the outcry raised against the Act was of quite a different origin. It arose from the provisions requiring the removal of blacks to reserves set apart for them, where the white man may not enter, and exempting only such blacks (or half-castes) as shall be employed under permit from the Protector of the district. These provisions were resented by the employers of black labour, and so misrepresented to the race they were meant to protect as to take on the aspect of a new tyranny. And indeed believed, it was conceivable enough that an indiscreet protector or inspector might work them to the needless injury both of black and white.

REPORT OF THE PEARL-SHELL AND BÊCHE-DE-MER FISHERIES COMMISSION.

In 1897, the commission was appointed on the motion of the hon. member for Cook, Mr. Hamilton and consisted of Mr. Hamilton, Mr. Dawson, Mr. O'Connell, Mr. Hoolan, and Mr. Smythall, members of the Legislative Assembly. It was appointed to inquire into the general working of the laws

---

[122] Qld Parl. 1898 V & P Vol. IV p 499.

regulating the pearlshell and bêche-de-mer fisheries in the colony. In addition to the report, the commission had supplied a considerable number of recommendations, no less than thirty-one in number, which included the following:

PACIFIC ISLANDERS.

89. It is not considered desirable to perpetuate the differentiation between the Polynesian employed in pearl shelling and other nationalities besides "native labourers." Polynesians have hitherto formed the intermediate class between the two extremes of intelligent aliens and dense-headed Binghis. Employers should be permitted to ship Polynesians like those aliens for two years, and to discharge them at any port in Queensland not further south than Townsville.

NATIVE LABOURERS.

90. An extension of the period for which native labourers can be engaged is clamoured for. The present maximum term is three months and is clearly insufficient for any business purposes. The prolonged term asked for by most witnesses is twelve months. The Commission, however, think that doubling the period to six months will meet present necessities without opening a door to oppression of 'native labourers'. Murray Islanders and the natives of other Straits islands need no inclusion among the "native labourers" specially safeguarded by law. They are quite as intelligent as Polynesians, and fully understand the nature of a shipping agreement. Many of them can read and write. The mainland natives require protection respecting their terms of hiring and their being returned to their ports of shipment.

BÊCHE-DE-MER AND TORTOISE-SHELL.

99. A witness conveyed the impression that certain abuses in the bêche-de-mer trade run perilously close to kidnapping, and are wrongly debited against the pearl-shelling trade. His opinion was that bêche-de-mer and tortoise-shelling should be kept distinct from the Pearl Fishery.

100. Bêche-de-mer fishing and tortoise-shelling are chiefly carried on by "native labourers." With this alarm respecting "kidnapping" still vibrating, repetition will not be redundant concerning the necessity for rigidly insisting that every "native labourer" must be returned to his port of shipment and that every "native labourer" found on board any vessel must be satisfactorily accounted for by the person in charge.[123]

The Aboriginals Protection Act was responsible for a mild excitement in shipping circles and had it not been for the prompt and determined action of Sub-Inspector Cooper, the bêche-de-mer fleet, which had its headquarters at Cairns, would have gone out of business. The vessels always employed aborigines as divers for the fish, and, according to the usual custom, the *Curlew* and *Dauntless* had signed on a number of boys, and were prepared to sail, when a telegram was received by Mr. Forbes from Dr. Roth, of Cooktown, as follows: "I am instructed to stop aborigines being shipped to the Coral Seas. Understand *Dauntless* and *Curlew* are under articles for Coral Seas. Detain them." As the Sub-Inspector is a Protector of Aborigines in this district, this wire was sent to him, and he at once telegraphed to the Commissioner for

---

[123] Qld Parl. 1897 V & P Vol II p 1301ff.

Police stating that he had given the two vessels permits to take aboriginals under section 17 of the Act, and repeating Dr. Roth's telegram. The Commissioner for Police, who is Chief Protector of Aborigines, at once wired back stating that Dr. Roth was acting under a misunderstanding and that if the Sub-Inspector and the shipping master were satisfied, the vessels might proceed to sea. The Chamber of Commerce also wired the Home Secretary with regard to the matter and received a reply in similar terms to that sent to Sub-Inspector Cooper. The two vessels left port accordingly.[124]

THURSDAY ISLAND REPORT FOR 1896 & 1897.

Relations established between the mainland natives and their employers continued to be fairly satisfactory. There had been no serious outrages. Occasionally natives had run away with boats, but in all these cases the boats were recovered. Sometimes the offenders gave themselves up for punishment. In other cases, they were frequently detected when they came up again for shipment. There had been several cases of woman stealing, but it was difficult to sustain prosecutions on such a charge. Under the new Aboriginals Protection Act, there was now no difficulty in establishing cases when they occurred. The Aboriginals Protection Act gave ample powers to remedy the abuses which used to prevail. The provisions of this Act itself were not very applicable to this district, but if worked in conjunction with the Native Labourers Act of 1884 they would prove effective. The appointment of Dr. Roth as Protector for the Northern and Central districts provided a good guarantee that the Act will be applied humanely. Moreover, it will be

---

[124] *Morning Post* 28 April 1898 p 5.

administered through the Commissioner of Police, which provided a further guarantee that it will be effective. Those clauses of the Act which referred to the sale of opium were put in operation here after a fair warning had been given. They at once put an end to the unwholesome and demoralising practice.[125]

REPORT OF THE COMMISSIONER OF POLICE ON THE WORKING OF "THE ABORIGINALS PROTECTION AND RESTRICTION OF THE SALE OF OPIUM ACT, 1897."

W. E. Parry-Okeden reported on 27 September 1898 as follows:

> Visits were also made to various other localities—among them Normanton and Thursday Island. At the latter place much good is being achieved, with the cordial cooperation of the hon. John Douglas and the shipping master, and by the harmonious working of The Native Labourers' Protection Act of 1884 with the Aboriginals Protection Act. Except those working about the island, most of the natives are employed on vessels engaged in the pearlshelling or bêche-de-mer trade. Dr. Roth, under date 6 May, writes:
>
> "I visited Thursday Island and consulted with the Government Resident and the shipping master, Mr. Bennett. The sergeant of police, McCreery, was too ill in bed for a prolonged conversation.
>
> No women, or children under puberty, are allowed to be shipped, although there is every reason for believing that

---

[125] Qld Parl. 1898 V & P Vol. I p 421ff.

the women are picked up again on the sandbanks from some thirty to fifty miles down the eastern coast of the peninsula. Bennett is keeping a sharp lookout for such offending employers, but until we can get a smart patrol steamer these gentry cannot be brought to justice. The Government Resident will also, in view of your telegram of 26 January, refuse permits for any aboriginals to be shipped on articles trading to New Guinea or outside Queensland waters. Furthermore, both in the opinion of the Government Resident and the shipping master, the island natives (i.e., those beyond Prince of Wales and Horn Islands) can understand English, are well able to take care of themselves, and do not require protective legislation—a fact which I was very pleased to learn, as my work will be only too fully occupied in dealing with the abuses to which the mainland natives are exposed. All aboriginals employed on the boats have, of course, to be on articles.

It would appear that just lately at Thursday Island there has been quite a revival in pearlshell surface diving, and it is probable that even more blacks than those already employed (about 300) will be required. At present they are being recruited principally from the western coast of Cape York Peninsula, along that tract of country known as the 'Seven Rivers'—i.e., the coast district between the Jardine River and the Batavia."

At the various police stations in the Peninsula, the police have been doing everything possible to encourage and protect the blacks in following their natural pursuits, and a feeling of mutual goodwill is being established.

Appendix A

Cooktown, 1 July 1898.

Sir, I report to you on the working of the above Act during the past six months, that its provisions have been carried out with as little friction as possible that the proper employment of aboriginals has been encouraged, and that particular attention has been directed to the discovery and suppression of existing abuses. In the Cook district, upwards of 1,100 permits have been granted and sixty refused; at Thursday Island six aliens were permitted to ship aboriginals, two aliens being refused. I am pleased to state that the Hon. John Douglas at Thursday Island reports, with regard to this act that "everything is working smoothly". Inspector Marrett at Cooktown speaks in the same strain, and Sub-Inspector Cooper at Cairns states that "the Act is working well without friction," and Inspector Graham at Normanton reports in similar terms. For reasons of which you cannot be unaware, all women, and, in the main, children under puberty, have been refused permission to be shipped on the pearlshelling and bêche-de-mer boats. W.E. Roth.[126]

THE HOME SECRETARY RETURNS FROM THE NORTH — ABUSES IN THE PEARLING INDUSTRY.

The Hon. J. F. G. Foxton, Home Secretary, returned on 9 August 1899 from an extended visit to the extreme Northern portions of the colony and the Torres Strait.

---

[126] Qld Parl. 1898 V & P Vol. IV p 499ff.

The abuses of the natives in connection with pearlshelling undoubtedly exist to a very large extent. The recruiting of mainland natives is principally for what is known as swimming-diving. The natives are very expert at that. I found that serious abuses exist regarding the recruiting of these men, and also in the treatment of native women and girls by abduction and violation, resulting in the spread of disease among them. The recruiters who commit the offences are very often Manilla men, the owners of luggers. The treatment of the Aboriginals on the boats is often due to want of knowledge on the part of the Aboriginals as to what they are going for, and when their hiring ceases. On first hiring, they have no idea of the meaning of time. An engagement means a hiring for six months. Sometimes the natives steal a boat to make off in their natural desire to be free, and sometimes they return with the boat after they have been to their homes.

Under proper regulation, the employment of the natives can be made to work for their benefit, and for the benefit of the industry. It enables the natives to earn money, and, under proper restrictions, is good for them if their wages can be assured them. The signing on is conducted with great care, and Mr. Douglas goes to very considerable trouble to see that the men are not paid cash, but their wages are handed over to the police, who go round with them, and make such purchases as they require, and get value for the money; but, notwithstanding that, they sometimes arrive at the mission stations empty-handed. I think I shall be able to remedy that. It is estimated that at least 300 natives are employed in the pearling industry. The trouble with respect to the women is that they are taken away in the boats, the owners alleging that they are with their husbands. That must be controlled in some way. On the general effect of the missions, and the work of the native police under Mr. Parry-Okeden's new system, Mr. Foxton said: In the mission stations the blacks seem to behave well. There is a wonderful improvement in their bearing towards the whites generally in the Cape York Peninsula. We shall probably hear of no more concerted attacks on white men. If crimes are committed, they will be personal affairs, like the crimes of white men. The new system inaugurated by Mr. Parry-Okeden with regard to the Native Police is working splendidly. The blacks regard the native police now as their friends and protectors.[127]

ABORIGINALS PROTECTION AND RESTRICTION OF THE SALE OF OPIUM BILL 1899.

Hon. J. F. G. Foxton in introducing the Aboriginals Protection and Restriction of the Sale of Opium Bill of 1899 said, in the administration of the Act of 1897 there have been found many points on which difficulties had arisen in connection with the duties imposed upon protectors of aboriginals, and it was now proposed by this Bill to give those protectors enlarged powers in order that more complete control may be obtained for the benefit of the employers, and for the protection of the aboriginals against harshness and various abuses to which a race such as they are liable, not only by our own race but also at the hands of alien races who largely employ these aboriginals in the North in connection with the pearling. It was found that The Native Labourers' Protection Act of 1884 did not make it necessary that the permit of a protector of aboriginals should be obtained prior to the employment of an aboriginal. It was proposed to alter that and make it quite clear that no one, under any circumstances, could employ an aboriginal without

---

[127] *Brisbane Courier* 11 August 1899 p 7.

the consent of a protector. This was a point on which the two Acts clashed, and it was proposed to amend the Aboriginals Protection Act accordingly. Another evil which frequently happened was, that men who employed aboriginals took them to another district and did not return them to their district. They were regarded as aliens by the members of the first tribe they came in contact with, and, perhaps, lost their lives. It was, therefore, proposed that recognisances should be entered into and proper securities given for the return of the aboriginals to their districts, if their employment necessitates their being taken from that district. Foxton also proposed further and additional housekeeping matters that would be reflected in the amended act.[128]

On 30 July 1901 in the Assembly, Hon. J. F. G. Foxton said, "this Bill for the most part was familiar to most hon. members who were in this House in the session of 1899, in which year it was read a second time and passed this Chamber, but came to an untimely end owing to a certain amendment proposed in the Legislative Council, which amendment I was unable to accept because it would practically have undermined the original Act of 1897. There have been a large number of cases brought under my notice during the last three years which indicate that, especially in the North and extreme North-west of the colony, the aboriginal population did not receive the benefits from the legislation which was passed in 1897 which it was intended by Parliament they should receive."[129]

The Aboriginals Protection and Restriction of the Sale of Opium Act, 1901 was assented to by his Majesty and proclaimed on 3 May 1902. The principal amendments Foxton sought were set

---

[128] Hansard LA 26 September 1899 p 117-118.
[129] Hansard LA 30 July 1901 p 208.

out in section 10 of the 1901 Act:

> No aboriginal or half-caste shall be employed under the provisions of "The Native Labourers' Protection Act of 1884," without the permit of a Protector granted in that behalf under the provisions of the Principal Act and this Act. And such permit shall be produced by the master of the vessel to the shipping master in whose presence the agreement of hiring is signed.
>
> No person shall employ on board of or in connection with, or suffer or permit to be upon, any ship, vessel, or boat, any male aboriginal who has not arrived at puberty, or any female aboriginal or female half-caste, unless under a written permit given by a Protector: Provided always that no female aboriginal or female half-caste who has not been tribally or otherwise lawfully married shall be employed upon any ship, vessel, or boat.
>
> A Protector shall not grant a permit for the employment of any aboriginal or half-caste on board of, or in connection with any ship, vessel, or boat trading, fishing, pearling or voyaging outside the territorial waters of Queensland.
>
> When any aboriginal or half-caste employed on board of or in connection with a ship, vessel, or boat is discharged at any port the employer shall, in addition to the payment of his wages, pay to the shipping master at the port of discharge a sum which such shipping master considers sufficient to defray all expenses of returning him to the place from which he was brought for the purpose of being engaged.[130]

---

[130] Aboriginals Protection and Restriction of Sale of Opium Act 1901 (2 Edw VII, No. 1)

REPORT OF THE NORTHERN PROTECTOR OF ABORIGINALS FOR 1899.

On 1 July 1900, Dr. Roth forwarded his report to the Home Secretary's Department on the recruiting and employment of blacks in the pearl shelling and bêche-de-mer industries:

> On the eastern coast of the Peninsula, from its northern extremity to a long way down—certainly as far as the Thursday Island recruiters would care to go—the Aboriginals are, speaking only as a matter of comparison, able to take care of themselves. I do not imply that they are on as high a scale of civilisation as the Torres Strait islanders, but having been so long used to the presence of the boats, they know what drink is; they recognise and appreciate the monetary value of their women; they suffer markedly with venereal disease; they have picked up the vices of their visitors, with the result that they are rapidly diminishing in numbers; and, from a practical point of view, too much "protection" on my part, though checking abuses, will probably not prove of much permanent benefit to them.
>
> On the western coast of the Peninsula, I recognise three distinct recruiting areas, each requiring separate notice: The 1st, from the Cape to Port Musgrave; the 2nd, from Port Musgrave to Albatross Bay (Duyfken Point); the 3rd, from Albatross Bay to beyond the mouth of the Archer River. The present consideration of the first may be dismissed for the reason that the same remarks as have already been referred to the Aboriginals of the east coast apply with equal force to the blacks on this portion of coastline.

With regard to the third, I may mention that the natives here are mostly myalls not too safe to travel amongst and that in the absence of contact with civilising influences, they can neither understand nor speak English; consequently, no recruits are obtainable here except by stratagem. It simply means that if unscrupulous people remove boys from here, the next to come will run greater chances of meeting with outrage. Being, therefore, only too anxious to take every precaution to prevent such occurrences, I have taken the safest means at my disposal to remove all those causes which I know from experience to be likely to give rise to reprisals. The recruiting in this particular area has accordingly been practically put a stop to.

The second and main recruiting area, especially in its relations to the two adjoining Mission Stations, Mapoon and Weipa, has occupied my grave anxiety and attention. The Hon. John Douglas had already instructed that all people recruiting here were to produce the written approval of Rev. N. Hey, the missionary at Mapoon when bringing the boys up to Thursday Island for signing on articles; he had stipulated that aboriginals were not to be worked on the boats for periods longer than six months at a time; he had spared no efforts in the attempt to get the boys returned to their native homes on expiry of their articles; he had arranged for the proper expenditure of their wages. From a legal point of view, unfortunately, much of the Government Resident's humanitarian action was ultra vires, and so it came to pass that his confidence in the recruiters became grossly abused, and his voluntarily self-imposed labours in the interests of the aboriginals practically emasculated. Cases occurred in which boys were signed on without the letter; others, where they had been taken from their homes without either the knowledge or consent of the missionaries and slipped past the island without being signed on. Often, the blacks were never returned at all.

Concerning the circumstances connected with the actual recruiting of the boys in this same district, I found that, under pressure from the old men, many of them were being bought and sold like so many sheep. The value locally of such a boy was a bag of flour and a pound of tobacco: at Thursday Island it was about 30s., the price which, as far as I could ascertain, was paid to the recruiting agent by the owner on whose boat the lad would then be shipped. The additional hardship lay in the fact, that it was not the young recruits who obtained the flour, &c., but the old men. They bringing the pressure to bear in getting the younger folk to ship: the corollary was that, in their absence, the old people got the pick of the women left behind, an occurrence which always gave rise to subsequent quarrelling. Indeed, it was in the personal and selfish interest of the aged males that the younger ones should be kept out of the way as long as possible. I obtained absolute proof (already reported) that boys were thus being recruited against their will.

As the result of careful investigation among the blacks, still referring to those inhabiting this same portion of coastline, I found that the pearling and bêche-de-mer industries, as formerly carried on, had been proving injurious to the aboriginal population in two ways: directly, in the high mortality amongst the younger males engaged on the boats, and indirectly in removing any chances of increasing the already low birth rate amongst the women left behind.

It is now a matter for sincere congratulation that since the appointment of the missionaries-in-charge as Superintendents of the Mapoon and Weipa Reserves, and the induction of a Protector of Aboriginals at Thursday Island an improvement is noticeable in the condition of affairs above alluded to. Mr. G. H. Bennett, the local protector, is keeping a sharp lookout for any abuses on the boats during his periodical trips, especially by seeing that the crews are all legally engaged and well fed, by attending to any complaints that may be made, and insisting that no women shall be carried. He tells me that owing to his determination of limiting the articles to a maximum of six months, there has been a marked decrease in the number of desertions. Other checks on the occurrence of abuses amongst the aboriginals employed on boats down the eastern coast of the Peninsula will be offered by the supervision with the patrol boat now in course of construction.[131]

Walter E. Roth, B.A., M.R.C.S., Northern Protector of Aboriginals, before the bar of the Legislative Council on 8 October 1901:

> A large portion of my time is devoted to the interests of aboriginals on boats. There used to be a great many cruelties and wrongs going on in the bêche-de-mer and pearlshelling industries; but, fortunately, with the help of Mr. Bennett, the shipping master at Thursday Island-who also happens to be the local protector for the

---

[131] Qld Parl. 1900 V & P Vol. V p 531ff, abridged.

Somerset district-we have minimised many of the abuses which used to take place. To assist in the work, the Home Secretary has very kindly allowed me the use of a cutter, the *Melbidir*, with which I patrol the whole coastline from Mackay to Burketown. During the present year, this has already been patrolled twice between the Wellesley Islands and Cooktown, and I propose continuing it from Mackay northwards next week. Of course, my work is much assisted by being appointed an inspector under the Pearlshell and Bêche-de-mer Fishery Act, as that enables me to bring into court a great many cases which it would be impossible to do as a protector of aboriginals. The captain of the *Melbidir* is similarly an inspector under the Pearlshell and Bêche-de-mer Fishery Act, and hence the work can go on whether I am on board or not. The remainder of the year, I spend on land getting in touch with the various local protectors. We exchange views, and often, they have a better idea concerning a local matter, and in that case, I give way and follow their views. I started this year from Cooktown in April, and have already seen personally nine out of the ten protectors who work under my instructions.[132]

To assist the reader in getting his head around the Pearlshell and Bêche-de-mer Fishery industry, the following statistics from the Shipping Office, Thursday Island, are provided for 1901. Participation rates were 10 floating stations, 4 tenders, 220 diving boats using pump and gear, 100 swimming diving boats, 5 tortoise shelling boats, and 11 bêche-de-mer boats generating revenue of £1382 to government in fees paid for boats. The gross returns to investors and operators were for

---

[132] Hansard LC 8 October 1901 p 1136. For a contrary view see the *Queenslander* 8 November 1902 p 1013.

pearlshell exported from Thursday Island £105,403; for bêche-de-mer £7399; and for tortoiseshell £2711. Labour levels in the industry at Thursday Island were as follows:[133]

Number of Men on Articles at the Shipping Office, Thursday Island.

Nationality of Employee	Number
Japanese	551
Malays	207
Manilla men	253
Torres Strait Islanders	285
Rotumahs	81
Samoans	15
Binghis	160
New Guinea (Papuan)	211
Europeans	67
Others	80
Total	2188

As Protector, Roth controlled Aboriginal labour exclusively. As an inspector under the Pearlshell and Bêche-de-mer Act, he had absolute power to stop, enter, search and detain any vessel and then to prosecute;[134] and he had the practical means to enforce his various powers by the use of his vessel the *Melbidir*. So, in the scheme of things, Roth well and truly had the bêche-de-mer industry by the short and curlies.

---

[133] *Brisbane Courier* 1 March 1902 p 14. Please note these figures do not include returns from Cooktown, Cairns, Townsville, etc. See also the 1890 report of Mr. W. Saville-Kent at p 67 above.
[134] Sections 6 & 10 of the Pearl-Shell and Bêche-de-Mer Fishery Act 1891.

Mr. A. Meston (South). Dr. W. E. Roth (North).
THE QUEENSLAND PROTECTORS OF ABORIGINALS.

State Library of Queensland

2

Assessment

The question is who, why, how, and when did indigenous elements collide with vessels and mariners within the maritime jurisdiction of Queensland, and what was the manner and method (form) of this interaction as to time, place, or other circumstances attending the incident; what was the evidence for the indigenous contact?

Remembering at all times, that the frame of reference is the nineteenth century and that Queensland was 8,921 nautical miles from its marketplace of London; and its mainland coastline length is 6973 kilometres together with an island length of 6374 kilometres.[135] That the mode of communication and transport was shipping via the Torres Strait, other than voyages to the Americas or the Pacific Islands; and the principal means of propulsion for the shipping in question was wind-driven or steam.

The type of shipping that plied the Queensland waters of the day was invariably described as Queensland, English, and European shipping, which might be better labelled as coastal, international, and transit. These terms are perhaps a little clearer:

---

[135] Geoscience Australia.

coastal means vessels trading[136] with or between colonial ports and islands; international meaning trading to or from overseas ports; and transit means vessels passing through Queensland waters.

After the data was collected, the first step was to select those marine incidents, within the relevant period, 1859 to 1901, which involved indigenous persons. Four indigenous groups emerged from the data: mainland Aboriginals, Torres Strait Islanders, New Guinea natives (Papuans), and Pacific Islanders (aka Kanakas or South Sea Islanders). For this book, and because of the complexity of the issues associated with New Guinea natives and Pacific Islanders in the colonial history of Queensland, I have excluded that data from the study; notwithstanding, I would have liked to have been able to compare and contrast the treatment of each indigenous group within the framework of Queensland colonial history.

The data collected, which forms part of this study, is set out in Tables 1 and 2 at pages 150 to 157 below.

The next step was to examine the activity of the vessels involved in the indigenous marine incidents. It was found that two types of activity emerged from the data, Bêche-de-mer fishers and Other. The category Other consisted of a broad range of activities. However, irrespective of the activity, when a vessel within this group, for whatever reason, found themselves shipwrecked, windbound, or with shore parties on the Queensland foreshore or coastal islands, they were attacked by Aboriginals domiciled at the place of anchor or landing.

---

[136] Trading includes commercial activities such as fishing and/or transporting cargo/passengers, etc. & etc.

Assessment

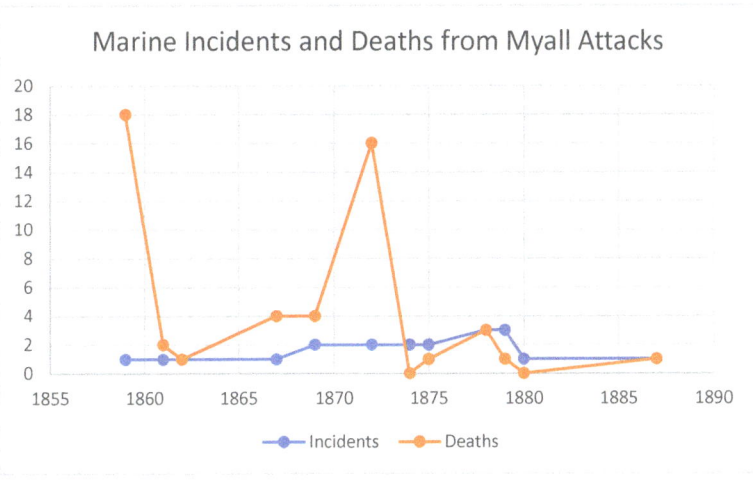

Graph 1 — Category Other

In the category Other, see graph 1 above, for the period 1859 to 1901, there were 20 marine incidents involving Aboriginals and Torres Strait Islanders.[137] From the 20 incidents, 50 white men and one Aboriginal were killed by indigenous elements as they intercepted the mariners who were either shipwrecked or members of shore parties. Invariably the bodies of the deceased mariners were eaten and at no stage did the indigenous elements ever communicate or warn the Queensland authorities of their intention to attack inshore or shipwrecked vessels. For mariners, Aboriginals simply became another hazard to shipping when sailing in Queensland coastal and island waters. In the absence of an explanation for their behaviour towards mariners, the only inference to be drawn is that their

---

[137] Marine incidents are complex matters involving human error, mechanical or material failure, bad or extreme weather, unknown navigational hazards, criminal acts, acts of God, etc & etc. However, this study is restricted to indigenes as either initiators or victims.

actions were predatory and murderous.[138]

I pause here to remind the reader that the Black Armband school of thought requires the historian to interrogate and decode colonialist historical narratives in favour of the indigenes. As a consequence, this injunction often leads followers of the Black Armband school of thought to put across absurd cultural excuses for brutal and savage acts of violence by Aboriginals not only against whites but tribal and clan members as well.

The reader is referred to Tables 1 and 2 to review the empirical data.[139] The data does not support the Black Armband school of thought that hostile attacks by Aboriginals on European vessels and crews can be interpreted as insurgency or military resistance, which is often described by leftist historians as guerrilla warfare.[140]

To illustrate the mentality of the Black Armband Brigade, I give an example of their extraordinary mental reasoning to avoid attributing criminal acts to myall blacks:

> Indeed, the first recorded fatalities from Aboriginal attack in North Queensland occurred on the sea frontier when two men on board the *Ellida* were killed at Shaw Island in the Whitsunday group after they had foolishly

---

[138] It is upon the same foundation of common right, that a free passage through countries, rivers, or over any part of the sea, which belongs to some particular people, ought to be allowed to those, who require it for the necessary occasions of life; whether those occasions be in quest of settlements, after being driven from their own country, or to trade with a remote nation, or to recover by just war their lost possession. Hugho Grotius, *On the Law of War and Peace*, Batoche Books, Kitchener, 2001 p 81.

[139] See pp 150-157.

[140] The History Wars is a tiresome subject much driven by left wing historians pursuing a political agenda of destroying the colonial history of white Australia while advancing the political aspirations of an Austral métis (Anglo-Aboriginal) alleging indigenous bloodlines.

placed themselves at the mercy of an Aboriginal group whom they had then unintentionally alarmed.[141]

Here is another ideologue dealing with the *Ellida* incident:

> He (Dalrymple) failed to mention that boat crews habitually fired upon natives and abducted their women or that he and Lieutenant Powell of the Native Mounted Police had both recently harassed the local 'savage' in punitive raids of unrecorded ferocity or discrimination.[142]

When the narrative of the *Ellida* incident is read alongside the above justification or excuse given by Messrs. Loos and Evans for the blacks' criminal acts, the reader will be forgiven, if he concludes that Loos and Evans are nothing more than apologists. Their left-wing cant and humbug are put forward to advance the political agenda of the Austral Métis.[143]

Bêche-de-mer Industry

Turning now to the Bêche-de-mer industry, over which so much controversy has raged concerning the management and workplace practices of the industry. Within the relevant period, 75 marine incidents occurred in which 124 persons were either killed, murdered, or missing at sea by the actions of myall blacks, binghi crews, or other persons.[144]

---

[141] Noel Loos, *Invasion and Resistance, Aboriginal-European relations on the North Queensland frontier 1861-1897*, Australian National University Press, Canberra, 1982 p 124.

[142] Raymond Evans, Kay Saunders, Kathryn Cronin, *Race Relations in Colonial Queensland a History of Exclusion, Exploitation and Extermination*, University of Queensland Press, 1993, 3rd Ed, p 28.

[143] Austral métis are the Anglo-Aboriginals of the twenty-second century who loudly proclaim their dispossession and oppression.

[144] Other persons is a mixed-race category and it cannot be assumed that as a class they were exclusively white men.

Number of Deaths by Cause

Race	Myall	Binghis	Other persons	Total
European/White	9	32	1	42
Asian	5	10	nil	15
Kanakas	4	5	5	14
Binghis	1	6	46	53

Why the industry was considered so bad is hard to say. The obvious answer appears to be because of the number of work-related deaths at the hands of Aboriginal or binghi crew. Although I have not canvassed the pearl-shell industry in depth, the average reader might be aware that in the early years of pearl shell diving, many divers died from the bends or decompression sickness. At the time, the industry and the government had an imperfect understanding of the cause of these deaths through ignorance.[145] Like soldiers, the divers died in the course of doing their duty and it was, therefore, considered preordained and nothing further might be done other than to eulogise their devotion to duty. The concept of workplace health and safety did not exist at that time. Therefore, it might be inferred that moral or emotional standards were used when evaluating the worthiness of the bêche-de-mer industry. They were said to have employed all sorts of immoral and deceptive practices and usages in recruiting Aboriginal labour, exploiting them, and then abandoning them.[146] Further contributing factors were that masters were coloured or Asiatic and that they cohabited with the Aboriginal women in a form of prostitution.

---

[145] Note: 1896, 19 divers died and as at October 1897, 22 had died, Pearlshell and Bêche-de-mer Fisheries Commission, Qld Parl. 1897 V & P Vol II p 1301ff.

[146] N.A. Loos, Aboriginal Resistance on the Mining, Rainforest, & Fishing Frontiers, Aboriginal European Relations in North Queensland 1861-1897.

To that end, the masters of the vessels were considered the scum of the earth. Whether bêche-de-mer fishers were, indeed, scum of the earth and moral degenerates it is hard to say. The data is silent on these matters.

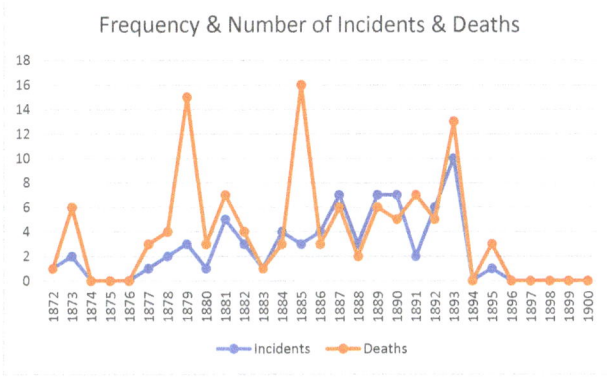

Graph 2 — Bêche-de-mer Industry

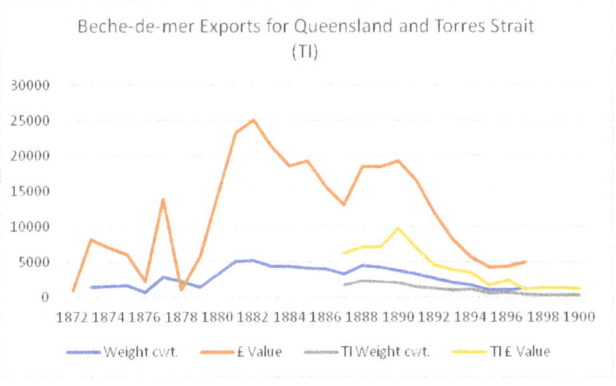

Graph 3 — Bêche-de-mer Industry

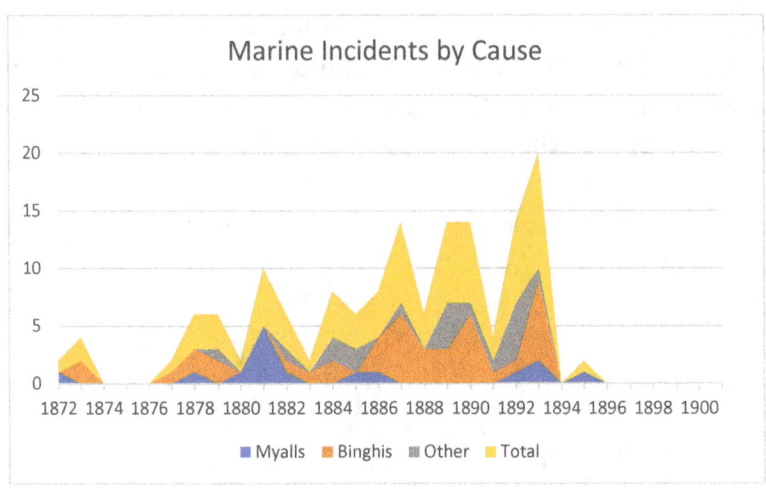

Graph 4 — Bêche-de-mer Industry

The big bogey of the time was slavery and enormous steps were taken by governments, particularly the Imperial government, to avoid any possibility that coloured labour might be employed or placed in circumstances of slavery. No attempt was made to manage the risk associated with engaging wild natives (myalls) for labour; the employer did that at his peril. However, employers could not man-steal or kidnap a wild native and sell him into slavery. Consequently, much attention was given to the proof of genuine consent by the native to the contract of labour or employment he made with the white employer. Notwithstanding this, the native was not familiar with the concept of labour contracting. Certainly, Aboriginals, given their pre-contact work practices, would have found some aspects of the labour contract difficult, such as the length of the contract and the meaningless repetitive nature of the work.[147]

---

[147] It is doubtful whether Binghis had any understanding of concepts such as work, remuneration, bargaining power, right to strike, etc & etc.

In the beginning, there was no regulation of labour, a master of a bêche-de-mer vessel was free to engage a mainland native, a Torres Strait native, or a New Guinea native. He was not bound by a formal written agreement of engagement with the native setting out conditions of employment. The master simply negotiated with the native ad libitum, and if the native was so inclined to work, came aboard and worked until he was released.

One marine incident stands out as having attracted considerable attention, the *Douglas* of 1877. The *Douglas* massacre has been highlighted by Noel Loos, one of the leading figures in the Black Armband Brigade of scholars, as an example of Aboriginal resistance.[148] On the other hand, the authorities of the time considered it an example of kidnapping natives. The master of the *Douglas* recruited three Aboriginal males from Dunk Island to mine and load guano from Chilcott Island onto the *Douglas* as cargo. Captain Harris said he held a license to hire native labourers and that the three natives were entered in the ship's logbook and were told they would get wages and rations. The evidence from the crew was that the hired Aboriginals didn't speak English and there was no sign of their wanting to leave the ship. On reaching the island the blacks did little labouring work and ultimately collected bêche-de-mer at low tide. Also at the island was the company's brig, *Alexandra*. The night after she left the island, the blacks attacked the crew of the *Douglas* and those who were on the island.

There was no statement by the blacks or evidence of motive for why they attacked and killed the crew. Moreover, the at-

---

[148] *Invasion and Resistance Aboriginal-European relations on the North Queensland frontier 1861-1897*, Noel Loos, ANU Press, 1982, pp 129 & 130.

tack was only stopped after two of the blacks were killed and the third jumped overboard. The inference is that the blacks intended to kill all of the crew. After the attack, the schooner, *Douglas* immediately sailed for Trinity Bay for help. The three badly wounded crew Shaw, Purcell and Deasy were transferred to the hospital at Cooktown for treatment of their serious wounds. On 22 February 1877, at Cairns an inquiry was held into the three murders and five charges of "with wounding", before Mr. E Morey PM and D Spence JP. It seems the statements of Shaw, Purcell and Deasy were not taken until late April 1877 at Cooktown by Water Police Magistrate B. Fahey and then forwarded to the Water Police Magistrate at Brisbane on 19 May 1877:

> Deasy, Purcell, and Shaw whose depositions I have taken were admitted to the Cooktown hospital on 24 February 1877. The two latter presenting a ghastly appearance from the mutilated state of the face, head, and body of each. They were discharged on 30 April their wounds healed but, although physically strong, their nervous systems fearfully shattered and bore permanent marks of bodily disfigurement.
>
> The abduction of natives from their Islands and haunts along the coast of Queensland by masters of pearl and bêche-de-mer fishing vessels, as well as those in search of guano and following various other pursuits has frequently resulted in the loss of life and valuable property and to this inhuman practice must undoubtedly be traced the murder of Coughlin, Mackintosh, and Troy by the natives taken by Capt. Harris from Dunk Island.
>
> This practice seems however, to have been hitherto carried

on with apparent impunity and as it cannot be justified by any law human or divine, I would respectively suggest it as a salutary means of preventing a repetition of such illegal and inhuman doings that the party or parties to whom the responsibilities of the *Douglas* massacre can be traced be punished and Captain Harris' conduct appears to have been not only unjustifiable but cowardly in the extreme throughout the whole melancholy affair.[149]

The Hon. W. Thornton, Collector of Customs and Water Police Magistrate at Brisbane added a memo of 28 May to the file and forwarded Fahey's depositions to the Premier via the Treasurer, which noted inter alia:

> I regard the conduct of the unfortunate blacks as above all praise. It contrasts strongly with the cowardness of the whites. Had three white men attempted to free themselves from bondage in the same way they would have been exalted to be heroes of the first order. The greatest share of the blame attached to this dreadful affair must rest with Mr. Beaver who no doubt was the instigator in the kidnapping. Much to be regretted if both he and Capt. Harris cannot still be legally prosecuted for their conduct.[150]

Although the above file is clearly marked that it was read by the Premier and the Attorney-General no action was taken against Captain Harris or the owners of the vessel. The incident appears to have been analysed by the magistrates in the following manner. Captain Harris kidnapped the Dunk Island blacks. The blacks after enduring bondage for at least a month

---

[149] QSA ITM 950296.
[150] QSA ITM 950296.

decided to kill all their white captors in a bid for freedom. If the blacks succeeded, at trial for murder they would have been acquitted on the ground of justifiable homicide. The difficulty with this legal analysis is that there was no evidence of the blacks being kept against their will. They never complained or requested to be returned to their homeland nor were they restrained in any way. More importantly, when the *Alexandra* sailed, they don't appear to have requested passage back to the Queensland coast.

In support of the above magistrates, BG Sheridan, Land Commissioner, Cardwell in a letter to government of 10 September 1877 made the following observations regarding Pearl and Bêche-de-mer Fisheries:

> At that interview, I ventured to bring under your notice the practice, which I trust is not common, of vessels engaged in the Pearl and Bêche-de-mer Fisheries in Torres Strait and-its-neighbourhood, kidnapping the natives along the coast and the adjacent islands, and forcing them to act as divers, &c. This offence is commonly known to the seafaring men frequenting the coast as "shanghai-ing them" (the natives). A notorious offence of this description was brought under the notice of the Government, in the case of the schooner *Douglas*, of Sydney.[151]

When Palmer introduced the Pearl-Shell and Bêche-de-mer Fisheries bill in 1879, he said it was introduced by the government to do away, as far as they could, with a good deal of irregularity and lawlessness which existed among the parties principally engaged in the pearlshell and bêche-de-mer fishery trade about the Barrier Reef, and the islands

---

[151] Qld Parl. 1877 V & P Vol. II p 1245.

that had lately come under the dominion of the colony. This bill provided for the employment and regulation of the engagement of Aboriginals.[152]

The Cooktown *Independent* provided the following observations on the bêche-de-mer industry as it stood at the end of 1887:

> The bêche-de-mer industry, which once employed a considerable fleet and a huge number of white and coloured men, has now dwindled to a very small proportion, the exports for the 11 months being only 95½ tons (1,910 cwt.), value £7871. The industry was taxed when it should have been encouraged, and instead of protecting the enterprising fisherman; the Government treated them as the 'kidnappers and murderers,' described by lying Missionaries, who thus encouraged the natives to 'wipe them out' until only a few are left.[153]

Mr. Saville-Kent observed in 1890, boat owners or their agents were assaulted and lost their lives, or boats with stores on board were stolen, which was so frequent as to paralyse the industry.[154]

The *Torres Strait Pilot* observed that when the mission station was formed in 1892, the natives became less inclined to work, becoming "educated" and lazy. Working for bêche-de-mer fishers became more irksome. It was not in the province of the missionaries to preach stern and speedy retribution if any murder was committed, or to instil into the chief the necessity to try and condemn any native who was guilty of a severe

---
[152] Hansard LA 1 September 1879 p 1523 & 14 July 1879 p 766.
[153] *Capricornian* 31 December 1887 p 8. Graph 3 above shows a sharp drop in bêche-de-mer sales in 1887.
[154] Saville-Kent report of 1890, see p 67 above.

crime and it is easily understood that the native soon drifted back to his old state of having no respect for the white man.[155]

The hon. Douglas observed in 1893, in response to the eight murders committed that year in the bêche-de-mer industry, that murder had been committed by the natives in pure revenge for personal injuries and insults. But in the majority of cases, the moving cause in the perpetration of outrages was the desire to return home. "But whether they were fed well or ill, whether they were treated badly or not, there came over them, long before the expiry of their legal agreement, an irrepressible desire to return to their own country and their tribal usages. They talk of this among themselves. Then they avail themselves of the first opportunity and knock him on the head or pitch him overboard. No good has come or can come from the Native Labourers Act in this district. Many white men have lost their lives at the hands of the natives".[156]

An interesting point of view was raised in a letter to the editor of the *Brisbane Courier* on 8 February 1894 regarding hon. Douglas' analysis of why the binghis resumed killing their bêche-de-mer masters:

> ...the work they (police) started before the mission came, and which brought about two years of absolute peace, was illegal, for it was an open secret they had known murderers punished by the natives themselves after a formal trial before the chief and the tribe. According to the police accounts, these trials were carried out with all the ceremony and pomp possible, to make them more impressive. With the mission at hand, illegal work by

---

[155] See pp 77-81 above.
[156] Report of Government Resident at Thursday Island for 1892-3, dated 1894. Qld Parl. 1894 V & P Vol II p 907ff.

men paid to see the laws respected could not be thought of. The knowledge of certain punishment when they returned to their native tribe being abolished, the natives soon commenced their murderous doings. This certainty of punishment will alone curb their "irrepressible desires." We presume this same "desire" existed during Mr. Savage's two years of peaceful rule or has it suddenly been created by the mission influence?[157]

Mr. A. Meston observed in 1896, that occasionally bêche-de-mer fishermen were killed by aboriginals driven to desperation, and most of these so-called "murders by the blacks" were merely acts of justly deserved retribution. The trade has been conducted by too many in a reckless, immoral spirit, free from any sense of responsibility, and neither amenable to nor fearing any kind of supervision whatever.[158]

Parry-Okeden, Commissioner of Police observed in 1897, that the bêche-de-mer business was a dirty one but profitable, and seemed to possess attractions for the lowest class of whites and Manilla men, who had no scruples whatever in dealing with their black employees. A master would sail from Thursday Island with two congenial ruffians (usually coloured men of nondescript nationality) as mate and cook. He would then by presents and promises induce as many blacks, male and female, as he can carry to come on board, and with them, he will make for any island as near settlement as he thinks safe. There he will land all the blacks except four or five males, with whom he will proceed to Thursday Island, and get them regularly shipped. Then taking all the male blacks, he would sail to a sandbank perhaps fifteen or twenty miles distant, where

---

[157] Page 7 of the *Courier*.
[158] A. Meston report of 1896; see pp 98-101 above.

the bêche-de-mer was to be collected. Eventually, the blacks would cast about for means of returning to their country; the master and his mates were suddenly tomahawked and thrown overboard, and the whole mob of blacks returned triumphantly to their country, having stripped and gutted the vessel.[159]

Graph 4 above shows a complete fall off in the bêche-de-mer trade from about 1894. In 1896, the *Cooktown Independent* observed that over 25 vessels, manned by over 300 Europeans and aboriginals, and representing nearly 200 more native employees, could have been counted in the harbour of Cooktown, all engaged in the bêche-de-mer trade, and of those only Matheson and Underwood remained. The murderous treachery of the aboriginals and Papuans helped to dispose of many, others abandoned the industry to spend the few hundreds they had made, while many were compelled to abandon the industry owing to the falling-off in returns for their labour.[160]

P. P. Outridge in giving evidence before the Pearlshell and Bêche-de-mer fisheries Commission of 1897 said:

> I do not recommend the engagement of binghis in connection with pearlshelling. I think the mainland natives should not be engaged in that industry. They suffer from the disease known as "nostalgia," and they commit all sorts of crimes to get back to their country.
>
> My opinion is that they should not be engaged in diving boats at all. The island natives are far superior to the mainland natives.[161]

Bêche-de-mer Marine Incidents

---

[159] Commissioner of Police report of 1897; see pp 101-104 above.
[160] *Week* 11 September 1896 p 20.
[161] Qld Parl. 1897 V & P Vol II p 1301ff, p 22 at 609 & 610 of report.

Marine Incidents Initiated by Myalls	Marine Incidents Initiated by Binghis	Marine Incidents Initiated by Others[162]
15 with 19 deaths	41 with 53 deaths	19 with 52 deaths

When the seventy-five bêche-de-mer marine incidents were examined as to type or category of indigenous interaction, it was found that 15 of the 75 incidents were caused by or attributable to myall blacks. These attacks were found to be predatory and murderous resulting in 19 deaths and thus, could be included in Graph 1 above and require no further comment.[163]

The next group of bêche-de-mer marine incidents totalled forty-one, which were caused by or attributable to binghis and accounted for 53 deaths.[164]

The question is why did the binghis kill the masters and crew of the bêche-de-mer vessels on which they worked with such regularity? As I indicated at the beginning, there are no Aboriginal sources on which one might rely to give an Aboriginal version of the events as well as an Aboriginal explanation of the events or a motive for their actions. There is not one account of the industry given by an Aboriginal who worked in the industry. Inquiries were held into the industry but no Aboriginal was called to give evidence. No European person was ever appointed to go out and conduct fieldwork amongst the Aboriginals who had worked on bêche-de-mer vessels so that a comprehensive study might be made of the industry relating

---

[162] Strictly speaking, it might have been better to have used the word, non-Aboriginals.
[163] See pages 125-129 above.
[164] Mainland Aboriginals were employed by masters of bêche-de-mer vessels to collect or harvest the animal from the reefs. In the industry, they were called Binghis. Strictly speaking they were not crew. They were analogous to a picker – someone who gathers crops or fruits etc. Some commentators alleged the word is offensive Australian slang.

to recruitment, pay and working conditions, workplace health and safety, and separation conditions from an aboriginal perspective.[165] Furthermore, no attempt was ever made to identify whether there were any Aboriginal cultural customs, practices, manners, or etiquette that may have clashed with the work patterns, practices, or procedures in the industry.[166]

The only evidence I have been able to find is from a marine incident in 1887. Captain Matheson of Cooktown took a crew of 29 binghis from the Mulgrave River in the schooner, *Spitfire* to collect bêche-de-mer at Conflict Island, Louisiade Group. He left two white men, Joseph McNair and Bethune, and Matthew, a native of New Caledonia, in charge of two boats and the twenty-nine binghis. On Matheson's return, Bethune advised him that McNair was dead; killed by Paddy. Matheson went to Paddy, who was in irons, and asked him, "What for kill Joe?"

Paddy said, "Me one fellow kill him, all other fellows talk, me kill him, also want kill two other fellows, take boat go home;" and that "Billy Barnton and Billy Cairns talk kill others."[167]

This incident might be confirmation of the industry view that binghis suffered from nostalgia, a need to return to country, and that they should not be kept away from country for long periods of time.[168]

The simplest way of looking at the issue is to view the attacks

---

[165] Saville-Kent, Meston & Parry-Okeden conducted surveys of the industry but they could not be called a qualitative study by ethnographers.
[166] For example, the Indian Mutiny, sepoys having to bite off the ends of cartridges lubricated with a mixture of pigs' and cows' fat.
[167] *Brisbane Courier*, 16 November 1887, p.5.
[168] See J Douglas's letter of 16 December 1893 at pp 82-84.

and killings as a labour problem. This was the approach taken by the colonial government of the time. Their initial view was that the bad behaviour of the Aboriginals was in response to the initial inappropriate behaviour of the bêche-de-mer masters when recruiting binghis for work parties. The 1881 Act required a binghi to be employed under a written agreement recorded in the Customs House or shipping office nearest to the place where it was intended to employ such labourer.

The 1884 Act provided that binghis were not be employed unless under articles; the agreement had to be explained and attested to in the presence of the shipping master; and the contents of the agreement had to contain the nature of the voyage and duration, maximum 12 months, job description, wages and scale of goods in kind. The binghis were also registered and given an identity disk.[169]

In 1890, the *Mackay Mercury* ran a series of editorials denouncing the bêche-de-mer industry because of the number of murders from 1888 to mid-1890 within the industry. In response to this newspaper reportage, the hon. J. Douglas, Resident, Thursday Island felt compelled to comment on the incidents. Some of his observations are worth quoting, "These binghi natives are most treacherous, and when they see a chance will inevitably take it." "In this case, I infer that Sadlier was not experienced in the ways of binghis. He was either too trustful or not watchful enough." Douglas concluded that no inspection or supervision was possible except at a large increase of public funds which could not be justified in the public interest and, further, the victims of the outrages were men who could not

---

[169] Native Labourers' Protection Act.

be refused licenses.[170] In other words, the masters of bêche-de-mer vessels were not reprobates.

The murderous outbreak in the bêche-de-mer industry of 1893 when 8 men were killed by the binghis, led the hon. J. Douglas to restate, "It (the bêche-de-mer industry) is impossible to supervise properly. To do so effectually would cost more than it is worth. I do not think that any good has come or can come from the Native Labourers' Protection Act of 1884 in this district. Many white men have lost their lives at the hands of the natives."

Of the remaining nineteen bêche-de-mer marine incidents, binghis were found to be victims with 52 fatalities. These marine incidents were predominately binghis missing at sea, 40 in total; with 6 killed by non-Aboriginal crew members. These 6 deaths were treated as criminal matters. Moncado was convicted of murder, and E. Moran was convicted of manslaughter while the other 4 deaths were not prosecuted.

What was the government's response to workplace difficulties in the industry? The government enacted an Act to make provision for the better Protection and Care of the Aboriginal and Half-caste Inhabitants of the Colony, and to make more effectual provision for Restricting the Sale and Distribution of Opium. This act effectively made Aboriginals wards of the state and regulated their daily contact with the white community. The act provided that whatever arrangements were made concerning the employment of Aboriginals the term of their servitude could not be longer than twelve months.[171] Dr. Roth, Northern Protector of Aboriginals observed, "I patrol

---

[170] J. Douglas to Colonial Secretary, 27 August 1890, Qld. Parl. V & P 1890 Vol. II p 1565.
[171] Hansard LA, 15 November 1897 p 1541.

the whole coastline from Mackay to Burketown. My work on the boats is much assisted by my being appointed an inspector under the Pearlshell and Bêche-de-mer Fishery Act, as that enables me to bring into court a great many cases which it would be impossible to do as a protector of aboriginals."[172]

Mr. Saville-Kent in his magnum opus, *The Great Barrier Reef of Australia; its products and potentialities*, finally summed up as follows:

> The aborigines from the Queensland mainland are extensively employed in this fishery, undoubtedly one of the few industries in which Australian native labour can be turned to profitable account. The native as a rule does not take kindly to agriculture or any manual work of a persistent character. There is not an employment that could be devised more to his liking than his attachment, accompanied by his wife and piccaninnies, to a liberally found Bêche-de-mer camp, with comfortable quarters, plenty of "tucker" and work which is to him almost his natural recreation. The attachment of the aborigines to fishing pursuits is practically demonstrated by the persistence with which the same families, or individuals, will year after year seek re-engagement at the hands of honest employers. Doubtless, many a tale could be told throwing discredit on their trustworthiness: tales of the massacres of station owners, of boats and stores, decamped with, and of the European or Manilla "boss" being marooned on a coral islet, or left to perish on a temporarily exposed reef. There is usually, however, an obverse side to these tragic pictures, which shows that

---

[172] Hansard LC 8 October 1901 p 1136.

the aboriginal was not the initial aggressor.[173]

W. E. Parry-Okeden, Commissioner of Police, observed:

No other people could walk and wade about the coral reefs collecting the fish as they do. They are unapproachable experts in the business, but their labour now, instead of doing them any good, is exploited for the benefit of unscrupulous ruffians, who pass their degraded lives in the indulgence of every form of vice at the expense of their miserable employees. The question of dealing with these employees and regulating the relations between these and their masters is distinguished from that of the non-seagoing aborigines by the fact that the existing shipping and fishery laws are ample for the purpose if thoroughly carried out, so that the whole matter is merely one of administration, and does not call for any legislative action.[174]

Noel Loos summed up as follows:

The sea frontier thus led to a multi-racial society not based on complete physical dispossession. The relationship between the fishermen and Aborigines was still one of colonizer and colonist, superior and inferior racial castes. This relationship also contained within it the seeds of exploitation by the dominant caste of the inferior caste and resistance by the inferior caste to the dominant caste.[175]

---

[173] Kent, W. Saville, *The Great Barrier Reef of Australia; its products and potentialities*, WH Allen & Co, London, 1893 p 228.
[174] Qld Parl. 1898 V & P Vol. IV p 499ff.
[175] Aboriginal resistance in North Queensland from Lectures on North Queensland History: Third series chapter 12 pp. 233-246 Loos, Noel A. Townsville, Qld. James Cook University, History Dept., 1978 p 243.

Examining the relationship between the industry and its Aboriginal workforce has only been possible when the industry has fractured because of Aboriginal indocility. I have used the word fractured because, if I had described the actions of the binghis as a walkout, strike, stoppage, withdrawal of labour, or industrial action, commentators would ask where is the evidence that the Aboriginal understood the concept of organised labour and that they were unionised.[176] The reality is that there is no evidence at all. The binghis did not understand the concept of production for consumption by a market.

Dr. W. E. Roth, Northern Protector of Aboriginals, was called to the bar of the Legislative Council, on 8 October 1901 and examined on the Aboriginals Protection and Restriction of the Sale of Opium Bill:

> By Hon. A. Gibson: Do you find aboriginals take kindly to agricultural pursuits?
>
> Walter E. Roth: No; that is the whole secret of it. The aboriginal is a nomad, and he reasons thus to himself: If by roaming for an hour in a day I can get my food for the next twenty-four hours, why should I work seven, eight, or nine hours for a white man?
>
> Q: Just now there is a difficulty in reference to coloured labour in the canefields. You say there are in your district 18,000 of those people, more or less. Do you think it would not be possible for the sugar planters of Queensland to employ them with advantage on the canefields for six or eight months of the year?

---

[176] Even as late as 1965 Aboriginals were not unionised; see equal wages for Northern Territory Aborigines, seeking to have the Cattle Station Industry (NT) Award amended to cover Aborigines.

Roth: The question is whether the blacks would be willing to do it. I have no right to force the blacks to work, although they are quite capable of doing it.

Q: Would money not induce them to take up employment of that description?

Roth: I do not think so. The blackboy notices that by working for an hour he can get food for the day, and he will not go to work for a whole day, except under compulsion. That is the difficulty; they are a nomadic people, not a settled agricultural one.

Q: You do not find the aborigines on the Johnstone River going in for working on the canefields?

Roth: As a rule, the blacks will not go in for labour of that kind.[177]

The Aboriginal made and used tools by his own hands within his habitat for his use. As Roth rightly pointed out above, Aboriginals were nomads not of the proletariat: not industrial wage earners who, possessing neither capital nor production means, earned their living by selling their labour. The bêche-de-mer master required the Aboriginal to move to a new location and use his labour to create something he did not need for a reward that he would receive some time in the future. From the Aboriginal perspective, this would have been outside his cultural experiences.[178] Their ready recourse to violence to solve their social and work problems suggests that they were

---

[177] Hansard LC 8 October 1901 p 1138.
[178] "...these people have never learnt to cultivate the earth and build houses, but remain content to wander about, living precariously on wild fruits, grubs, a little chance fish, and such animals as they can spear." *Surveys and Discoveries*, &c., Captain Moresby, R.N. p 18.

significantly disconnected from the workplace environment as well as suffering severely impaired communication and mediation skills. They were often described as treacherous. From a European standpoint, the binghis were a "poor cultural fit", but there was no other labour force available.

These bêche-de-mer camps or "sit-down country" proved to be locations of dissatisfaction where the Aboriginal workforce would, it appears, acutely experience or develop an intense feeling of isolation and alienation through pining and fretting for their home country. Consequently, the need to return to their tribal haunts and habitats, drove them, on occasion, to steal vessels and even murder their overseers. Employing binghis, as they were known, proved to be a challenging task, knowing that their unpredictability might at any time lead to an outburst of violence, which would not only terminate the contract of labour but also the life of the employer.

Consequently, what is related in the following pages is a brief description of the marine incidents as they came to the notice of the authorities of the day. As to the accuracy of the statistics, every effort has been made to record the material as faithfully as possible. The reader needs to keep in mind that the intent of the statistics is for indicative or illustrative purposes only. No warranty can be given as to accuracy and completeness. Of course, the following narrative is by Europeans who were charged with the supervision, control, and regulation of the Bêche-de-mer industry. The material reflects Eurocentric methods of thinking, governance, law enforcement, and social norms.

The History of Bêche-de-mer Fishing in Queensland Waters and Adjacent Islands

Table 1 – Torres Strait Islanders

Ship	Date	Location	Event	Remarks
Sapphire	23/9/1859	Sir Charles Hardy Islands	TSI killed 18 white crew on Hammond Is. & eaten	Shipwrecked, no provocation; Ranked with Hornet Bank & Cullin-la-Ringo as outrages
Sperwer	April 1869	Prince of Wales Island (Muralag Is)	2 crew murdered & eaten by TSI natives	Trading; predatory attack by hostile natives, poss. 6 killed

Table 2 – Aborigines.

Ship	Date	Location	Event	Remarks
Ellida	27/9/1861	Shaw Island	Myalls kill 2 white men	Predatory, windbound shore party, oystering
Presto	June 1862	North of Cape Palmerston	Myalls kill 1 white man	Predatory, shore party looking for water
Eva	March 1867	Hinchinbrook Island	Myalls kill 4 white people	Predatory, shipwrecked
Eliza	October 1869	Cape Grenville	Myalls kill 2 white men	Predatory
Unknown	12/1/1872	Gould Island	Myalls kill 2 white men	Predatory, fishermen
Maria	26/2/1872	Bramble Reef	Myalls kill 14 white men	Predatory, shipwrecked
Victor Emmanuel	1/10/1874	Burrow Island	Attacked by Myalls	Predatory, vessel oystering, looking for water
Albert Edward	6/6/1874	Palm Island	Myalls attempt to burn the vessel	Vessel sheltering, mixed with gins; myalls retaliated
Jessie Anderson	8/5/1875	Port Molle	Attacked by Myalls	Predatory, landed for water

Assessment

Unknown	23/10/1875	Jardine River	Myalls kill 1 Fraser Island Aboriginal	Predatory, landed for firewood & water
Unknown	August 1878	Lizard Island	Myalls attack Purdie	Predatory, landed to cook
Louisa Maria	10/8/1878	Whitsunday Island	Myalls kill 1 white man	Predatory, landed for water & careening boat
Riser	August 1878	King's Reef	Myalls kill 2 whites	Predatory, shipwrecked
Prospect	February 1879	Hinchinbrook Island	Attacked by Myalls	Predatory, landed for wood
Unknown	6/2/1879	North Beach, Cooktown	Sykes & Hartley speared by Myalls	Predatory, timber getting
Success	6/8/1879	Cape Melville	Myalls spear white man	Predatory, cedar getters
Pearl	23/6/1880	Archer River	Night attack by Myalls, repulsed	Predatory, exploring River by Capt. Pennefather
Chance	16/2/1887	Jardine River	Myalls kill white man	Predatory, prospectors

Aborigines and the Bêche-de-mer Industry Table – 3

Unknown	27/9/1872	Stanage Bay	Myalls kill 1 Chinese Loot station	Bêche-de-mer station, no provocation
Goodwill	12/4/1873	Green Island	Binghis kill 2 white men	Bêche-de-mer fishing, no provocation.
Florence	11/7/1873	Green Island	Binghis kill 3 white men, 1 kanaka	Bêche-de-mer fishing, no provocation
Douglas	January 1877	Chilcott Island	Binghis kill 3 whites and wound 5	Guano & bêche-de-mer, revenge for kidnapping
Captain Cook	22/3/1978	Dunk island	Myalls attack crew, 1 white wounded	Bêche-de-mer, looking for cedar logs on shore

The History of Bêche-de-mer Fishing in Queensland Waters and Adjacent Islands

Flying Scud	1/8/1878	Mulgrave Island	Binghis kill 1 white man, 2 Malays, and 1 Chinese	Pearl shelling, Port Essington blacks; revenge for kidnapping
Gem	5/8/1878	Mabuiag Is.	Binghis attack chief officer Mogg	Pearl shelling, Port Essington blacks; revenge for kidnapping
Spray	August 1879	Piper Lightship	10 Binghis missing at sea	Bêche-de-mer fishing
Bowen	14/8/1879	Piper Lightship	Johnson speared by binghis	Bêche-de-mer, binghis revenge Spray loss of binghis
Spray	27/10/1879	Raine Island	Binghis kill 3 binghi, 1 white, 2 Chinese	Bêche-de-mer fishing, no provocation
Unknown	25/12/1880	Newcastle Bay	Myalls kill 3 kanakas	Pearl fishing, landed to clean boat
Lady Denison	September 1881	Cairncross Island	Myalls kill 2 whites	Bêche-de-mer, landed for firewood, no provocation
Irish Girl	November 1881	Night Island	Myalls steal stores & guns of Capt. Webb	Bêche-de-mer station, no provocation
Unknown	November 1881	Flinders Island	Myalls attack Capt. Miller's station	Bêche-de-mer station, no provocation
Unknown	October 1881	Barrow Islands	Myalls kill 1 kanaka	Bêche-de-mer station attacked, no provocation
Mrs. Watson	29/9/1881	Lizard island	Myalls kill woman, baby, 2 Chinese	Bêche-de-mer station looted, no provocation.
Titfish	9/5/1882	Lizard Island	4 binghis missing at sea	Bêche-de-mer, due to alcohol

Assessment

Claremont Lightship	6/10/1882	Claremont Island	Myalls spear 1 white crew, recovered	Recovery of stolen bêche-de-mer boat
Unknown	November 1882	Cooktown	5 Binghis arrested for desertion	Bêche-de-mer station of Mr. Fuller
Samoa	19/10/1883	Warrior Island	Binghis kill white Capt.	Bêche-de-mer fishing, no provocation
Mary Lee	Feb 1884	Cape Flattery	Assaulting binghis	Bêche-de-mer, Capt. NG
Alarm	20/7/1884	Boydong Is.	8 Binghis missing at sea	Found at Margaret Bay
Unknown	July 1884	Green Island	Binghis abandoned Capt. on reef	Bêche-de-mer fishing, no provocation, crew survived
Ruby	25/7/1884	F Reef, Barrier Reef	Binghis abandon 2 binghis & white man on reef	Bêche-de-mer fishing, no provocation, presumed drowned
Annie	15/7/1885	Cape Upstart	Crew of 5 kanakas & 5 binghis missing	Bêche-de-mer fishing, missing at sea
Sin Wong Cha	June 1885	Lizard Island	1 white crew & 4 binghis missing	Bêche-de-mer fishing, missing at sea
North Star	29/7/1885	Restoration Is.	Myalls kill 1 white, some wounded	Bêche-de-mer fishing, no provocation
Rip	January 1886	Cape Flattery	Binghis kill white Capt.	Bêche-de-mer, Binghi jealous husband
Rover	April 1886	Barrier Reef	Binghis kill 1 binghi; 2 binghis speared	Bêche-de-mer fishing, no provocation
Echo	June 1886	Cape Bedford	Binghis abandon white man on reef	Bêche-de-mer, no provocation

Unknown	5/10/1886	Cape Melville	White speared by Myalls	Bêche-de-mer fisher, no provocation
Nellie	20/2/1887	Endeavour Reef	Cutter wrecked on reef	Bêche-de-mer, binghis rescued
Florence	21/2/1887	Archer Point	Binghis steal cutter	Bêche-de-mer, Supposed return to country
Coral Sea	June 1887	Cape Bedford	Binghis put whites overboard 1 died	Bêche-de-mer fisher, no provocation
Rotumah	11/10/1887	Hamilton Island	1 white crew killed by binghi over food	Bêche-de-mer fisher, no provocation
Lizzie	6/10/1887	Albany Island	Binghis kill Malay & attack Capt.	Bêche-de-mer fisher, no provocation
Fiji	18/10/1887	Barrier Reef	Binghis abandon black Capt. & mate	Bêche-de-mer fisher, no provocation
Spitfire	November 1887	Conflict Island	Binghis kill 1 white crew, return home	Bêche-de-mer fisher, no provocation, nostalgia
Petrel	May 1888	Cape Kimberly	Binghi kill white Capt.	Bêche-de-mer fisher, no provocation
Daluma	23/5/1888	Piper Islands	Christiansen, *Rover* charged with piracy	Bêche-de-mer, Christiansen discharged
Tam O'Shanter	August 1888	Batavia River	Binghis put Capt. Mogg overboard	Bêche-de-mer fisher, no provocation
Mary	November 1888	Batavia River	Vessel stolen by binghis	Bêche-de-mer fisher, no provocation
Irish Lass	23/1/1889	Cooktown	E Moran shot A. Byers, binghi	Bêche-de-mer fisher, Manslaughter guilty – life

Assessment

Wild Duck	March 1889	Barrier Reef	3 whites killed by kanaka & binghis	Bêche-de-mer fisher, Kanaka convicted-larceny; binghis discharged
Unknown	March 1889	Restoration Island	G. Dillon shot binghi, Harry	Bêche-de-mer fisher, Dillon acquitted
Unknown	18/7/1889	Warrior Island	Johnson shot binghi in self-defence	Bêche-de-mer fisher, committed but no true bill
Rotumah	12/7/1889	Thursday Island	John Williams sailed with 7 binghis	Bêche-de-mer, missing believed killed by binghis
Peg	12/6/1889	Claremont Isles	Binghis steal *Peg* & desert	Bêche-de-mer, no provocation
Mecca	3/1/1890	Sir Charles Hardy Group	Binghis killed Pratt & stole *Mecca*	Bêche-de-mer, no provocation
Ada	April 1890	Cape Grenville	Billy Wilson beaten by binghis	Bêche-de-mer fisher, no provocation
Alice, lugger	May 1890	Haggerstone Island	Burstow & Maynard attacked by binghis	Bêche-de-mer station, no provocation
Annie, lugger	May 1890	Haggerstone Island	Charlie Weir, kanaka murdered by binghis	Bêche-de-mer, no provocation
Jenney Scott	October 1890	Coral Sea	Capt. Robinson 3 gins not on articles	Bêche-de-mer, fined £5 for each gin & costs
Ruby, cutter	31/10/1890	M Reef	Binghis kill Capt., mate & kanaka	Bêche-de-mer, over gins, binghis discharged
Alert	8/12/1890	Warrior Island	Binghis steal lugger	Bêche-de-mer, return to country, Alert recovered
Rover, schooner	20/4/1891	Geraldton (Innisfail)	Binghis abscond	Bêche-de-mer, Capt. obtains warrant for arrest

Carbine	26/7/1891	Green Island	7 Binghis missing presumed drowned	Bêche-de-mer, Binghis missing on reef fishing
Unknown	9/1/1892	Little Woody Is	Binghis steal cutter	Turtle-sheller, no provocation
Unknown	28/2/1892	Red Island Point	Binghis discharged on beach, 2 die	Bêche-de-mer, binghis abandoned
Skitty Belle	23/5/1892	Thursday Island	Moncado murdered Bob, Darwin binghi	Pearling schooner, binghi sodomised by Moncado
Warrill	11/4/1892	Two Isles	Mouri, a binghi shot dead	Bêche-de-mer, Underwood drunk, no true bill filed
Resolute	11/6/1892	Fairway Buoy	Sandy, a binghi shot dead by white crew	Bêche-de-mer, binghi put off, killed in self-defence
P.C.E.	November 1892	Cockburn Islands	Myalls loot Pim's station	Bêche-de-mer, no provocation
Blackfish	29/12/1892	Thursday Island	Binghis not on articles	Bêche-de-mer fisher fined £10 plus costs
Curlew	January 1893	Barrier Reef, Bowen	Binghis abandoned by Capt., dispute	Bêche-de-mer fisher, Capt. to be prosecuted
Unknown	13/5/1893	Forbes Island	Binghis kill George Waters	Bêche-de-mer fisher, no provocation
Leonora	27 May 1893	Seven Rivers	Binghis kill Manilla men Kintu, Pascual	Bêche-de-mer, no provocation
Miranda	1/6/1893	Bathurst Bay	Myalls kill 2 Japanese crew	Bêche-de-mer, no provocation
Blackfish	24/6/1893	Boydong Cay	Binghis attack 3 Manilla men, 1 died	Bêche-de-mer fisher, gins involved

Assessment

Unknown	October 1893	Burke Island	Binghis threw H. Nicholls overboard	Bêche-de-mer, another binghi saved Nicholls
Alice, lugger	18/10/1893	Mapoon	Binghis kill Mobeck & Oien	Bêche-de-mer fisher, binghi dispute over flour
Wren, lugger	November 1893	Skardon River	Binghis kill C Bruce & S Rowe	Bêche-de-mer, no provocation
Beryl	November 1893	Night island	Myalls kill Greenlaw & Jones	Bêche-de-mer, no provocation
Darn	26/11/1893	Batavia River	Binghis steal lugger	Bêche-de-mer, no provocation
Violet	December 1895	Clerke Island	Myalls kill 2 white men & binghi	Bêche-de-mer, no provocation

BIBLIOGRAPHY

1908 Queensland Pearl-Shell and Bêche-de-mer Commission. Report of the Royal Commission Appointed to Inquire into the Working of the Pearl-shell and Bêche-de-mer Industries.

Carroll, J. M., Ed., *Journey into Torres Straits*, Queensland Heritage, volume 2 issue 1.

Cilento, Sir Raphael with the assistance of Clem Lack, Ed., 1959, Triumph in the tropics: an historical sketch of Queensland, The Historical Committee of the Centenary Celebrations Council of Queensland, Brisbane, Qld.: Smith & Paterson.

Dillon, Paul, 2020, Inside the Killing Fields: Hornet Bank, Cullin-la-Ringo & The Maria Wreck, Connor Court Publishing, Brisbane.

Evans, Raymond, Saunders, Kay & Cronin, Kathryn, 1993, 3rd Ed, Race Relations in Colonial Queensland a History of Exclusion, Exploitation and Extermination, University of Queensland Press.

Falkiner, Suzanne & Oldfield, Alan, 2000, Lizard Island: the journey of Mary Watson, Allen & Unwin.

Ganter, R. 1994, *The Pearl-Shellers of Torres Strait*, Melbourne University Press, Victoria.

Ganter, Regina, 1998, *Living Immoral Lives - Coloured Women and the Paternalistic State*, Hecate Press.

Ganter, Regina, 1999, *Letters from Mapoon: Colonising aboriginal gender*, Australian Historical Studies, 29:113.

Grotius, Hugho, 2001, On the Law of War and Peace, Batoche Books, Kitchener.

Johannes, R.E. and MacFarlane, J.W. 1991, *Traditional fishing in the Torres Strait Islands*, CSIRO Division of Fisheries, Hobart.

Kent, W. Saville, 1893, *The Great Barrier Reef of Australia; its products and potentialities*, WH Allen & Co, London.

Loos, Noel A., 1978, *Aboriginal resistance in North Queensland* from Lectures on North Queensland History: Third series chapter 12, Qld. James Cook University, History Dept.

Loos, Noel, 1976 Aboriginal-European relations in North Queensland, 1861-1897. Ph.D. thesis, James Cook University.

Loos, Noel, 1982, *Invasion and resistance: Aboriginal-European relations on the North Queensland frontier 1861-1897*, Canberra: Australian National University Press.

McNiven, Ian J. 2018, *Ritual Mutilation of Europeans on the Torres Strait Maritime Frontier*, The Journal of Pacific History, DOI: 10.1080/00223344.2018.1499007

Moresby, Captain John, 1876, Discoveries & Surveys in New Guinea and the D'Entrecasteaux Islands, London: John Murray.

Mullins, S. 1992, *Queensland's Quest for Torres Strait: The Delusion of Inevitability*, The Journal of Pacific History, Vol. 27, No. 2.

Parnaby, O. 1964, *Britain and the Labor Trade in the Southwest Pacific*, W Duke University Press, Durham, N.C.

Paterson, Lance, 2003, *Wreck-ollections: ships & shipwrecks in Queensland waters*, Vol. 1.

Robertson, Jillian, 1981, Lizard Island: a reconstruction of the life of Mrs. Watson, Hutchinson of Australia.

Sharp, Nonie, 1992, *Footprints Along The Cape York Sandbeaches*, Aboriginal Press Studies, Canberra.

The History of Bêche-de-mer Fishing in Queensland Waters and Adjacent Islands

The History of Bêche-de-mer Fishing in Queensland Waters and Adjacent Islands

www.ingramcontent.com/pod-product-compliance
Lightning Source LLC
Chambersburg PA
CBHW051317230426
43669CB00032B/2696